The Praise of God in the Psalms

THE
PRAISE OF GOD
IN THE
PSALMS

By Claus Westermann
Translated by Keith R. Crim

JOHN KNOX PRESS
Richmond, Virginia

LIBRARY OF CONGRESS CATALOG CARD NUMBER: 65-10553

© M. E. BRATCHER 1965

PRINTED IN THE UNITED STATES OF AMERICA

2074-WB-7457

Contents

Explanations of the Abbreviations

THE PSALM CATEGORIES

LP: Psalm of Lament of the People
LI: Psalm of Lament of the Individual
PP: Declarative Psalm of Praise of the People
PI: Declarative Psalm of Praise of the Individual
P: Descriptive Psalm of Praise
EP: Eschatological Song of Praise
DW: Double Wish (explained p. 52, note 1)

APOCRYPHAL AND PSEUDEPIGRAPHICAL WORKS

1 and 2 Macc.: 1 and 2 Maccabees
Pr. of Man.: The Prayer of Manasseh
Add. Dan.: Additions to Daniel
Ecclus.: Ecclesiasticus, or the Wisdom of Jesus the Son of Sirach
Ps. Sol.: Psalms of Solomon
Od. Sol.: Odes of Solomon

THE SOURCES OF THE BABYLONIAN PSALMS

K: Texts from the British Museum (Kujundschik)
KAR: *Keilschrifttexte aus Assur religiösen Inhalts* (Ebeling)
KAT: E. Schrader: *Die Keilinschriften und das A.T.*
KM: L. W. King, *Babylonia Magic and Sorcery,* being "The Prayers of the Lifting of the Hand," 1896 (also being abbreviated as King Mag or BMS)
LSSt: *Leipziger semitistische Studien*
IR, IIR, etc.: H. Rawlinson, *Cuneiform Inscriptions of Western Asia,* London
VAT: Vorderasiatische Abteilung der Museen zu Berlin, Tontafelsammlung

OTHER ABBREVIATIONS

A.T.: Old Testament (in German works)
O.T.: Old Testament
N.T.: New Testament
ZAW: *Zeitschrift für die alttestamentliche Wissenschaft*
BZAW: Beihefte of the *ZAW*
BWANT: *Beiträge zur Wissenschaft vom Alten und Neuen Testament*
HSAT: *Die Heilige Schrift des Alten Testaments*, eds. Feldmann and Herkenne, Bonn
KHSAT: E. Kautzsch, *Die heilige Schrift des Alten Testaments*, 4th edition, ed. Bertholet
OTS: *Oudtestamentische Studien*
HAT: *Handbuch zum Alten Testament*
RGG: *Die Religion in Geschichte und Gegenwart*
VT: *Vetus Testamentum*

Preface

In the present transitions and disasters the church has been confronted anew with the question of the praise of God. Praise has played a limited role in the relationship of modern man to God. The last time it had real significance was in the period of the enlightenment, but it was then essentially praise of the Creator. Only recently, and only in those places where the church was under severe trial has the praise of God been again awakened. A collection of letters from pastors of the confessing church, which were illegally printed during the church struggle, bore the title: . . . *And They Praised God.* A pastor collected poems from the years of the church struggle and the war in a volume: *Praise Out of the Depths.* At about the same time there appeared outside the church a volume of poetry from the same period with the title: *De Profundis.* In many places, even including the gathering of a congregation at the side of the grave, this new tone can be heard.[1]

Here and there under the heavy burden of what was happening to them, members of the congregation discovered that they were not only learning patience and self-discipline under that which had been given them to bear, but that *under* the burdens, despite all trials, they were able to praise God. For all who experienced it, it was a real discovery that this was possible.

In such praise out of the depths, their need, the sorrow through which they had to struggle all alone, was no longer merely their own concern. It was not *merely* a test and confirmation of their piety, a happening that took place between God and their soul, but it was an occurrence in the congregation.

1. K. Barth, *Credo*, p. 124: "Praise of God is the most endangered and the most dangerous undertaking of the church. Everyone can praise, even the heretic! Thus it must be that at certain times one speaks but little or not at all of the praise of God, that there are special times when it awakens with power and then is neither endangered nor dangerous."

Whenever one in his enforced separation praised God in song, or speech, or silence, he was conscious of himself not as an individual, but as a member of the congregation. When in hunger and cold, between interrogations, or as one sentenced to death, he was privileged to praise God, he knew that in all his ways he was borne up by the church's praise of God. By this it became an element of what was going on between God and the world. At all times and in many places there have been men who suffered and died for their convictions. In the accounts of the Acts of the Apostles it is clear that the strongest outward impression is made by the fact that the witnesses of Jesus Christ sing and praise God in prison. By this they make known that God acts, whatever may happen to them. Something of this forensic[1a] character of the praise of God has again broken through in our time. This praise out of the depths has become an argument that speaks louder than the arguments that we have been accustomed to bring forth for "Christendom." As such it became a sort of exegesis of Holy Scripture. (Compare Gerhard Ebeling, *Kirchengeschichte als Geschichte der Auslegung der Heiligen Schrift* [Church History as the History of the Exegesis of Scripture], Tubingen, 1947. See especially p. 24.) The church is to be open at this point, to ask and to hear. What about this praise out of the depths, what about the praise of God in any case?

The question concerning the praise of God has yet another side, which is posed for the church in a wider horizon by the liturgical movement, in interconfessional contacts and discussions. It is the whole question of cult. Both questions, that of the praise of God in the trials of the church and that of the praise of God in the "liturgy," have encountered each other in a strange way in recent German church history. In part they run along beside each other, and in part they are remarkably intertwined with each other.

The great number of questions that are here only alluded to are to be attacked exegetically at one point: What is the praise of God in the Psalms?

1a. "Forensic" is used here in the simple meaning, "public, occurring in public."

Their proper "Yes" to God, which they have in common in contrast to that which is today historically powerful, the existential (in the pregnant meaning of the word) "No" to God, is not primarily to be found where someone says something about God or his relationship to God, but where he turns to God.

In the introductory paragraphs of his *Old Testament Theology*, L. Köhler says of God's being, "The deeper one descends through the centuries into the breadth of the Old Testament writings, the louder the praise and laud of God can be heard. But they are not lacking even in the oldest pages, and each act of praise is a confession of the ever-present sentence—that God is" (pp. 1 ff.).

Today our history bids us inquire about it anew. The following undertaking which investigates the praise of God in the Psalms is intended to help in this inquiry.

Preface to the Second Edition

Since the book is out of print and there is still demand for it, it is now appearing, thanks to the friendly willingness of the publisher, essentially unaltered in a second edition. A lack of time prevents me from undertaking now a revision that would take into consideration the literature that has since appeared (especially the Psalm commentary of H.-J. Kraus, which was published in the interim), or to deal with the objections which have been raised. I would not need to change anything on the essential lines which the work follows. The objection has repeatedly been raised that the designations "declarative" and "descriptive" Psalms of praise (instead of "song of thanks" and "hymn") are too complicated. I readily admit this, but so far no terms have been suggested to me that are simpler or more accurate. I am not concerned with the designations as such; the traditional ones may simply continue to be used. My essential concern is to make clear through these terms that they are both categories of the praise of God, but that they are to be clearly distinguished from each other as different ways of praising God. I have found wide agreement that what takes place in the declarative Psalms of praise cannot be unambiguously reproduced with our word "thank." If F. Mand ("Die Eigenständigkeit der Danklieder als Bekenntnislieder," ZAW, 1958, pp. 185-199) wants to take the songs of thanks as "songs of confession," I will agree with him that the Hebrew hōdāh contains the element of confession. I once suggested that one could say confessional praise instead of declarative. Nevertheless, because of the entirely different sound of our words "confess" and "confession," it must be clearly expressed that hōdāh in any case contains that element which we can reproduce only with "laud," "praise."

To be sure, the group of Psalms that I have brought together

as "descriptive Psalms of praise" have throughout that characteristic that is meant by this designation and are thereby clearly distinguished from the "declarative"; still there is need for a more
exact differentiation (according to an oral suggestion from R.
Rendtorff). In this area further work has been done on individual
Psalms in the interim. An exact grouping of these Psalms, which
would take into consideration both their particular function for
worship and the elements of tradition which are recognizable in
them, has not yet been made. What has been said in my work of
this whole group of Psalms of praise was intended to bring out
only a few lines which are important for their exegesis, but it is
not adequate for the exact determination of the individual
groups and types. Now as before, I regard the way in which this
whole complex of Psalms of praise is throughout determined by
the polarity of the majesty and the condescension of God as the
essential matter. Illustrations of this can be freely multiplied
from Second Isaiah, Job, and many individual passages.

The literature which has appeared in the meantime in the
treatment of this research cannot be cited in detail. Rather
reference should be made to the bibliography in the Psalm
commentary of H.-J. Kraus, which appeared in 1960 (*Biblischer
Kommentar,* Neukirchen, Vols. 1 and 2). This material is collected at the end of the introduction, and then is also found in
connection with the various Psalms. In addition, reference should
be made to the very valuable collection by J. J. Stamm, "Ein
Vierteljahrhundert Psalmenforschung" (*ThR,* NF 23, 1955, pp.
1-68).

C. Westermann
February, 1961

PART ONE

The Categories of the Psalms

What does it mean in the Psalms to "praise God"? An exhaustive answer to this question cannot be found simply through an investigation of the vocabulary of praise as it occurs in the Psalms.[2]

Indeed, this investigation must take second place. The words for praise are to be found to an astonishing degree, more so than any other verb in the Bible, in the imperative (including the voluntative, cohortative, and jussive). The greatest part of this vocabulary, therefore, exhorts to praise.[3]

Praise takes place in words. This can occur in two ways. A teacher who wants to praise a pupil can say to him, "I praise you!" But we immediately feel that this is not the real way to praise. It sounds wooden, stiff, pedantic. But the teacher can also say, "That was well done!" This is the real way to praise (of course there are many possible forms it may take). In that sentence, then, praise *occurs*.

This real way of praising, in words or sentences that do not even contain the word "praise," is also present in the Psalms. We thus are confronted with the question, which are these words or sentences in the Psalms in which God is praised? What do *they* say to us about the praise of God in the Psalms?

This is the question concerning the categories in the Psalms: In which Psalms is God praised? Only in recent times has re-

2. This must be reserved for special investigation.
3. The expressions "I praise . . ." or "we praise . . .," which are frequent in our liturgies and hymns, are not encountered in the O.T. prior to the work of the Chronicler.

15

search into the categories become a serious undertaking. At the
end of this development stands Gunkel's *Einleitung in die
Psalmen,* which, after his death, was completed and published
by Begrich (Göttingen, 1933). In this book the results of the
form-critical work on the Psalms are united in a masterful whole,
which enables us to see all the comprehensive range of the structure of the Psalms in their various categories, from the basic
forms to the most distant branches, which grow out of the given
elements of form into ever new variations.

According to Gunkel (pp. 27, 30), the major categories of the
Psalms are the following:

> Hymns
> Laments of the people
> Laments of the individual
> Songs of thanksgiving of the individual
> "Spiritual poems" ("the real treasure of the Psalter").

In addition there are smaller categories, including the "songs of
thanksgiving of Israel" and the "Torah."

With this may be compared Kittel's "Introduction" (D. R.
Kittel, *Die Psalmen,* 1929); he was already acquainted with and
approved of Gunkel's earlier work:

> The hymn (song of praise)
> The prayer of thanksgiving
> The prayer of petition
> The didactic poem
> The spiritual song (as highpoint of the poetry of the
> Psalms).

The distribution is, apart from minor differences, identical.
Some typical examples of earlier attempts to divide the Psalms
into classes are given in Gunkel's work ("Introduction," pp. 8 f.).

In Gunkel, as also in Kittel, Hempel, and others, the "hymn,"
the Psalm of praise, stands in the first position. This is not entirely obvious. At first glance the Psalms of petition are certainly
more numerous (Kittel: "prayer petitions"; Gunkel: "laments of

the people," and "of the individual"). Gunkel occasionally refers
to the great significance which the "hymn" apparently had (pp.
83, 433: the hymns are "the most important part of the collection"). This is seen especially in that this category had the greatest influence on other—actually on *all* other—categories, although Gunkel does not specifically establish this. Later it must
be asked whether this formulation entirely fits the facts. In any
case Gunkel asserts again and again throughout his entire work
that the "hymnodic" (can one say this?), hymnodic elements,
small hymns, are encountered everywhere in the other categories.
This wide-reaching influence cannot be established for any other
category. Thus here the priority of the "hymn" over all other
categories is clear. In the survey it stands with good cause in the
first place.

Now, however, the unbiased reader of Gunkel's "Introduction"
notices a remarkable irregularity. Why is it that songs of thanksgiving are not divided into those of the people and those of the
individual as the laments are? Gunkel has a category "songs of
thanksgiving of Israel" (pp. 64, 265, 315) and includes it among
his "smaller categories" (p. 315, no. 28). On page 315 he explains
their small number by the tendency of the human heart, which,
after deliverance, forgets to thank the helper.[4]

The same reason also explains to him why the songs of thanksgiving of the individual are so much fewer in number than the
laments (p. 235). The remark, however, that the "songs of thanks
of Israel" are related to the hymns, leads in another direction.
Indeed, "such songs of thanks and hymns merge into one another:
Pss. 65:1-8; 66:5-12; 67; 75" (p. 64). This agrees with the presentation of the "songs of thanks of Israel" individually and as a
special group among the enumeration of the hymns, p. 32. So
Gunkel too really counts them as hymns.

In the same way, the boundary between the "songs of thanksgiving of the individual" and the hymns is a fluid one. The definition on page 272, "To sing a song of thanks means to proclaim

4. Essentially the same reason is given by Balla, *Das Ich der Psalmen*, Göttingen,
1912, p. 66, and is taken up by Joh. Döller, *Das Gebet im Alten Testamente*, Wien,
1914, p. 51.

Yahweh's grace before all the peoples," defines, as will become
clear, precisely not a song of thanksgiving, but a hymn! Gunkel
deals explicitly with the mixture of style with that of the hymn
on pages 272-274. The remark on page 276 is decisive: "The dif-
erence is that the songs of thanks shout for joy (note this verb!)
over the specific deed which God has just done for the one giving
thanks, while the hymns sing the great deeds and the majestic
attributes of God in general" (cf. p. 83).

Does not this observation say quite clearly that there exists
between hymn and song of thanksgiving really *no* difference of
type, or category, and the song of thanks, of the individual and
of the people, is really another type of hymn? The result is then,
that in the Psalter there are two dominant categories, the hymn
(including the Psalm of thanks) and the lament.[5]

5. This comes very close to an old division of the Psalms represented by Hupfeld's
work (Hupfeld[2]-Riehm, *Psalmen* I[2], pp. 3 ff.: songs of praise and thanks, songs of
lament and petition, didactic songs).
    Merely in order to present material for reflection, I will here show at a few points
that Gunkel has not succeeded in clearly separating the two categories from each
other.
    The real meaning of the hymn is most clearly expressed on p. 70: "The hymn is
sung for God alone." Similarly on pp. 71, 72, 39, 41, etc. The meaning of the hymn
is lauding, praising, glorifying God. In the context where Gunkel recalled the
biblical term *tehillāh* (pp. 58 f.), he himself said once, "song of praise." And to
be sure, in a song of praise it is a matter of "the whole fullness of the majesty of
God," p. 41. The difference between hymn and song of thanks is described well and
clearly on p. 276. (Cf. the last quotation before this note.)
    According to this the two categories are clearly designated and distinctly separated
from each other. The "song of thanks" refers to a specific, unique act of God that
has just been experienced by the singer; the "hymn," to "the great deeds and
glorious attributes *in general.*" The two categories are distinguished, not by the
difference of the predicates but by the objects. It is not a question in them of different forms of speech, as asking and giving thanks are different, but the difference
lies in that which is spoken of. In any case it is thus clear that "hymn" and
"lament" are to be distinguished from each other in a different way than are
"hymn" and "song of thanks."
    The designations of the categories, however, give the impression that they are
intended to distinguish here and there the way of speaking. Here it should be asked
further, what then is the difference between "praising" and "giving thanks," and
what do they have in common? But this question does not permit the term "hymn"
to appear. In reality, Gunkel's way of speaking is determined generally not by that
good and clear distinction, but by the fiction of a "hymnodic" expression which is
differentiated from giving thanks. Here the hymn is raised to a higher plane. It
belongs to the hours of pious solemnity; again and again the word "mood" was
used (pp. 34, 68, 83, 178, 243, 276, 280, etc.), or "inspiration" (pp. 37, 48, 70, etc.),
or "awe and reverence" (p. 75). All these modern concepts are contained *in* the
vocabulary of praise. All these things exist for the men of the Old Testament only
in this total turning of man to God. The vocabulary and the phrases of the praise
of God are still strong enough to express this for him. But here Gunkel became
involved in insolvable difficulties.
    On pp. 79 and 84 the definition of "song of thanks" serves almost word for word

But just what is a hymn? In what realm does it belong? There are three possible answers to this question: It is a literary unit, or a cultic unit, or a mode of prayer.

In the various realms and phases of research that are concerned with the "hymn," one of these answers is always tacitly presupposed, without a real clarification having been reached.

In Heiler's great work[6] the hymn is one of the types, or main forms, of prayer. In this the literary hymn is understood as a development of the priestly cultic hymn, which was in turn preceded by the "primitive song of prayer." (It is significant that the concept "hymn" is avoided for this first step; apparently this means that only the song of prayer that has developed into a cultic or literary stage can be called a hymn!)

In literary investigations, the hymn is generally understood as primarily a literary form, as, for example, Hempel considers it.[7]

In Gunkel's introduction the literary and the cultic designation of the hymn are brought together. The hymn, as it is found in the sources, is first of all a literary document, and to this extent the term "hymn" designates a literary category. This category,

---

as that of a hymn. On p. 79 Exod. 15:21 is dealt with among other passages. On what grounds is this called a hymn? It corresponds exactly to his own definition of a song of thanks, which had just been cited. To be more exact, Exod. 15:21 belongs under the correct definition of a song of thanks of the people, p. 316, which agrees in the important particulars with the definition on p. 276. (I can only imagine that he let himself be misled through the introductory word *šīrū*, which is really the introduction of a "hymn." But the song also has been transmitted with another introduction, Exod. 15:1, "I will sing." [LXX reads, "Let us sing."])

At the beginning Gunkel said that the category could be recognized most clearly by the introduction (p. 25), but according to p. 83 the hymn and the song of thanks generally agree in the introduction and in the conclusion. (This is said more sharply on p. 267.) This confusion could have been avoided if Gunkel had maintained the distinction, according to which the two types can be clearly distinguished in the main part of the song. The "song of thanks" reports one specific action of God, and the "hymn" praises God's activity and his being for us in their fullness. In other respects Gunkel's assertion is only partially valid in the introduction, and in the conclusion only in rare and exceptional cases.

In other places where Gunkel spoke of the relationship of hymn and song of thanks to one another, the same thing happened. He spoke almost only of what they have in common. "Song of thanks and hymn have the same rules of form" (p. 251). He spoke often of their agreement in form (pp. 267, 274, 275, 276), and on p. 285 said the same thing of the Babylonian psalms. (1 Sam. 2 is called a song of thanks on p. 5, and on p. 32 it is included among the hymns.) But he also said that hymn and song of thanks agree in their basic mood (pp. 275, 267, 276). They are related to each other, p. 42, and they merge with each other, p. 64.

6. Fr. Heiler, *Das Gebet*, fifth edition, 1923.
7. "Die althebräische Literatur," Potsdam, 1930, pp. 30 ff.

however, does not have its real position in literature. Gunkel goes behind the literary stage and looks for the "Sitz-im-Leben": "What then was the Sitz-im-Leben of the Psalms? Judaism made use of them in the cult, as the term *tehillīm*, i.e., hymns, shows. The Babylonian psalms belong together with certain cultic practices. . . . Thus we may venture the supposition that they were originally derived from the Israelite cult." What is said here in the beginning of the Psalms in general, Gunkel said specifically for the hymns, p. 59, and for the other categories, pp. 175, 181, 182, 117, 260. Mowinckel then carried the cultic interpretation of the Psalms far beyond this approach of Gunkel's in a comprehensive investigation of the cultic bases of the Old Testament Psalms in their environment.[8]

This became the starting point for a new direction in research that explained not only the Psalms out of the cult, but also in addition vast areas of the Old Testament writings. For the Psalms, reference should be made on the one hand to Aage Bentzen's work (see the bibliography) for the development of this line of research in Scandanavia, and on the other hand to A. Weiser's introduction to his exposition of the Psalms in the new Göttingen commentary series as a representative example.[9]

This whole line of research has taken a road that has as good as forsaken the original question that was raised by Gunkel. In the foreground there now appeared the question concerning the cultic myth or the cultic ideology which generally stood behind the texts which were explained in terms of the cult. In contrast to Gunkel, who sought to grasp each of the Psalm categories in its peculiar character and its many-sided existence, a tendency became dominant which tried to fit everything into the same mold. It began with Mowinckel, who attributed about a third of all the Psalms (of the greatest variety of categories) to the en-

---

8. S. Mowinckel, *Psalmenstudien*, I-VI, Kristiania, Schriften der Wissenschaftsgellschaft, Histor.-philos. Klasse, 1921-1924. Cf. now S. Mowinckel, *The Psalms in Israel's Worship*, tr. D. R. Ap-Thomas, Oxford, 1962 (2 vols.).

9. An example of the cultic explanation of a complex from the historical books is to be found in Pedersen, *Israel, Its Life and Culture*, III-IV, London, 1940, Appendix I, pp. 728-737, where the account of the exodus from Egypt is explained as the historicizing of a cultic legend. An example of the invasion of the prophetic books by this explanation is Engnell, *The Call of Isaiah*, 1949, a study in which the author seeks to explain the call of Isaiah in terms of purely cultic elements. For further literature, see the surveys mentioned in the bibliography.

thronement festival which he discovered. And in Bentzen's area of research it led to the extreme results, wherein on the one hand practically all Psalms became royal Psalms, and on the other hand fundamental significance was ascribed to a cultic pattern which was held to be valid for the whole of the ancient East, and to be widely determinative for Israel's Psalms. The same tendency, moreover, is to be seen at work in milder form in Weiser's introduction to *The Psalms,* when he observes "that the cult of the covenant festival is to be assumed as the Sitz-im-Leben of the vast majority of the individual Psalms and their categories" (p. 18), and when he regards as the central point of this covenant festival the dramatic presentation of the theophany, reflexes of which are to be found in a large number of the Psalms.

This whole tendency to explain as many as possible or even all of the Psalms either by the "ideology" of a specific (and only just discovered) festival, by a cultic schema, or by the connection of a basic myth with a specific ritual (Hooke), seems to me, in spite of all the effort that has been expended on it in the last thirty years, to have produced meager results for the understanding of the individual Psalms. The concept "cult," which is basic for all the branches of this line of research, became in the process more limitless and confused. It is high time finally to ask soberly what is regarded as cult in the Old Testament and what the Old Testament says about cult. It will then be impossible to avoid the fact that in the Old Testament there is no absolute, timeless entity called "cult," but that worship in Israel, in its indissolvable connection with the history of God's dealings with his people, developed gradually in all its various relationships, those of place, of time, of personnel, and of instrumentality, and that therefore the categories of the Psalms can be seen only in connection with this history. All the work on the Psalms along the lines which Mowinckel indicated cannot excuse us from taking up again the task set for us by Gunkel of research into the individual Psalm categories in their development and in the history of their various component parts.

It is impressive to observe in Gunkel's work the way in which

the texts of the Old Testament resist with a strength of their own
our occidental concepts, which are the products of entirely different situations. For there, where Gunkel inquires into the
origins of the hymn which has its place in the cult, this concept
and this definition both fail him. Heiler also avoided the name
"hymn" for the earliest stage; he spoke there of a "prayer song."
In reality it is not a question here of a literary or of a cultic
hymn. Rather it becomes clear what the hymn is in its original
significance: praise of God.

On p. 89, in a section that begins with the assertion that
hymnody grew out of worship, Gunkel gave as three of the
oldest examples: the Song of Miriam, the Song of Deborah, and
the Song of the Seraphim in Isaiah 6. No one of these three can
be called cultic in the strict sense. The Song of Miriam and the
Song of Deborah (the latter belongs to the special category of
songs of victory) show, rather, with unmistakable clarity what
the Sitz-im-Leben of the hymn is: the experience of God's intervention in history. God has acted; he has helped his people.
Now praise *must* be sung to him.

Isaiah 6:3 is also no cultic song in the strict sense, but it is
nevertheless nearer to what is called cult. In what way is it different from the other two examples? The difference is clear and
almost leaps out at the reader: there it is a specific, single intervention of God in history which calls forth praise; here in Isaiah
6:3 it is God in the fullness of his being and his dealings with
the world. Those two have the structure, "Yahweh has done,"
and this, "Yahweh is."

Here Gunkel, without realizing it, placed side by side the two
basic types of the Psalm of praise in their earliest and simplest
forms: the declarative and the descriptive Psalm of praise. They
have in common the essential fact that in them God is praised.
There he is praised for a specific, unique intervention, and here
for the fullness of his being and activity.[10]

It is already clear in these two examples that the descriptive

10. This is precisely the distinction which Gunkel makes on p. 276 between a
hymn and a Psalm of thanks. See above.

Psalm of praise has a clearer affinity to that which is really cultic than the declarative does. The latter very clearly has its location "out there," in the midst of history, yes, while still on the battle-field—in the hour and the place where God has acted. It might be said that both were sung in a service of worship which was held after the battle, but it is obvious that such a service of worship has a different character from that which shines through Isa. 6:3. If these are both called "cultic," then this distinction is erased and the concept of the cultic, which was intended to include both, is already unusable from the start.

At the end of the same section, p. 89, Gunkel assumed "that Israel learned the art of hymnody as it gradually came to be at home in Canaan." After the three above-mentioned examples this sentence sounds very strange. In order to utter the words in Exod. 15:21 or Isa. 6:3 is it necessary to be instructed by another nation? Apparently Gunkel means here not these words but the great songs of praise, as for example, Judg. 5. It is certainly to be assumed that they were influenced by Babylon and Egypt, probably by way of Canaan.[11]

But in such statements the decisive element has been over-looked. It is not necessary to study how to praise God. The fact here is that a great deal depends on the terminology. Hymns can be learned. When this word is used one almost inevitably thinks of a fine, cultivated, artistic creation with harmony and euphony, that is, of a literary unit. Is that, however, what either of these two examples is intended to be? Is it not actually in-admissible to designate such a single, short sentence by the liter-ary term "hymn"? It is intended to be praise of God and nothing more. And the fact that the praise of God is something that can-not be learned is certainly an essential feature of this praise. To a certain degree the form that is given to the words can be taken over and learned, but the simple act of praise that can be comprehended in a single sentence would lose its genuineness and its significance if it were borrowed.

11. Gunkel's surmise was validated in relation to the Song of Deborah by the dis-coveries at Ras Shamra. Cf. N. H. Snaith in *The O.T. and Modern Study,* p. 94. Additional literature is listed there.

In another place Gunkel too sees that. Where he speaks of the Psalms, not as literary or cultic creations, but as prayers, he does not recognize such a literary or cultic dependence. On p. 261 Gunkel says of the question of the dependence of the Israelite Psalms on the Babylonian psalms, which agree with them so astonishingly, "Should we believe that before the time of the Babylonian influence in Canaan no one prayed to God amid the exigencies of life? Everywhere where a man raises his hands in prayer, the same component parts of prayer and the same sequence of these components appear. . . . Thus regarded, the relationship rests . . . on the peculiar nature of prayer as such."

Is that, however, not also valid for lament and petition? On pp. 282 f. Gunkel speaks of the relationship of the songs of thanks to the laments and says they "correspond to one another like the shells of a mussel," and after he has developed that, on p. 284 he says, "In the alternation between lament and song of thanks there unrolls the whole life of the pious." With this may be compared p. 181, ". . . they transport us into the midst of life, but not into the service of worship."

In these two sentences, which are astonishing in the light of Gunkel's basic thesis, recognition begins to dawn that somehow the observation that the life situation of the Psalms is the cult really cannot be right. For that which really, in the last analysis, occurs in the Psalms is prayer. Gunkel himself sees that here. There is a good reason why this recognition to some extent appears only in an occasional flash and then disappears again. What takes place in these Psalms as men turn to God is in essence something different from what we of the present day name prayer (thus Gunkel p. 47). It must be conceded that Gunkel was right in this. That which he designates as "hymn" somehow does not fit into our general concept of "prayer," for our concept of prayer is actually determined in its essentials by thanks and petitions. Does, however, Gunkel's statement which was just quoted, fit for the Psalms or for the entire O.T., where the whole life of the pious is passed in the alternation of songs of lament and of thanks? If so comprehensive a statement may be attempted, would it not be truer to the O.T. to say, between lament and *praise?* This would mean then that precisely in the place of our contrast of petition and thanks there stands in the O.T. the contrast of lament (supplication) and praise.

Therefore we must inquire into the relationship of thanks and of praise to each other.

PRAISE AND THANKSGIVING

The fact that there is no word for "to thank" in Hebrew has never been properly evaluated. The ignoring of this fact can be explained only in that we live so unquestioningly in the rhythm between the poles of thanks and request, of "please!" and "thank you!", and the thought does not occur to anyone that these concepts are *not* common to all mankind, have *not* always been present as a matter of course, do *not* belong to the presuppositions of human intercourse nor to those of the contrast of God and man. We are compelled to imagine a world in which petition plays a thoroughly essential and noteworthy role, but where the opposite role of petition is not primarily thanks but praise. And this praise is a stronger, more lively, broader concept which includes our "thanks" in it. Thanking is here included entirely within praise.

Perhaps it will be easier to understand this if we remind ourselves that even today none of our children learns on his own to express thanks. He has to be told a hundred times, "Say thank you!", and he still does not say it without being reminded. In addition, where the polish of good upbringing disappears, the expression of thanks soon falls by the wayside. In male society, the harder the life is, the less expression of thanks there is. I have established this point again and again in the war and as a prisoner. Even under the worst circumstances someone will always beg a cigarette, but he very quickly forgets to say thank you.

At the basis of this there is a linguistic process that has long been known, but which has a much greater significance than has generally been assumed. In primitive languages all the force and intensity of linguistic formations is found in concrete expressions. In the African languages there is an amazingly large number of verbs for the way a man walks, and they represent the many nuances of meaning in walking. On the other hand our so-called abstract words are here essentially more complex, for the differentiation is secondary. For example, "good" and "beautiful" have not been differentiated in טב, and depending on the context it can mean either. There are, however, other passages where the meaning should not be differentiated (as in Gen. 1). The same unity is still to be found today in the Russian хороший. In our modern languages there are whole lists of words for which there is, in Hebrew for example, no single corresponding word (for example, "modest"). And among these is "to thank." This word developed from a secondary differentiation of meaning, and what we mean by it was once contained in a verb that appears to us as complex. This is not hard to understand. A glance at our languages shows at once that this verb is not a primary formation. The German word is a variant of the verb *denken* (to think), and so is the English. In Latin it is a nominal formation, and in Greek a denominative from the corresponding noun (*gratia-χάρις*), which basically has a different meaning. At this point the Russian language is again interesting, where there is still used to express thanks a word that properly means "to give honor," благодарить. These references are enough to show that "to thank" is clearly a secondary formation in many languages. (I know of no language in which "to thank" has its own root.) It would appear then that it became an independent verb by a later development out of a more complex verb.[12]

In the Old Testament this differentiation has not yet taken place, and there is as yet no verb that means only "to thank." *Hōdāh*, which is usually translated as "to thank," is not used in the Old Testament a single time for an expression of thanks

---

12. H. Schurtz, *Urgeschichte der Kultur*, Leipzig-Wien, 1900, p. 186, refers to the primitive languages in which there is no word for "to thank." This is cited by Heiler, p. 44, where we read further, "This reminds one of the rich vocabulary of the Rigveda in which there is no word for thank."

between men. Thus it is clear from the start that this *hōdāh* cannot be equated with our "to thank," which can be directed equally to God or to man. In those places in the O.T. where our "thank" as something taking place between men is most clearly found, the verb used is *bērēk*, which does not have the primary meaning of "praise" but means "bless."[13]

In view of these facts, it is clear that the O.T. does not have our independent concept of thanks. The expression of thanks to God is included in praise, *it is a way of praising*.[14]

Thus Wendel in his investigation of lay prayer in Israel contrasts the prayer of petition or lament not with the prayer of thanks, but with the prayer of praise (p. 170).

Those elements which characterize modern thanks, now independent of praise, may be characterized briefly.

1. In praise the one being praised is elevated *(magnificare)*; in thanks the one thanked remains in his place.

2. In praise I am directed entirely toward the one whom I praise, and this means, of necessity, in that moment a looking away from myself. In thanks I am expressing *my* thanks.

3. Freedom and spontaneity belong to the essence of praise; giving thanks can become a duty.

4. Praise has a forum and always occurs in a group; giving thanks is private, for it need concern no one except the one thanking and the one being thanked.

5. Praise is essentially joyful; giving thanks can take on the character of something required. Praise can never, but thanks must often, be commanded.

6. The most important verbal mark of difference is that thanking occurs in the speaking of the words, "thank you," or in shortened form, "thanks"; genuine, spontaneous praise occurs

13. Examples are Deut. 24:13; 2 Sam. 14:22; Job 31:20; Neh. 11:2. The falling down of one person before another can have the meaning of thanks: Gen. 23:7, 12; 2 Sam. 9:8; 14:22; 16:4; 1 Kings 1:31; Ruth 2:10. Before God: Gen. 24:26, 48, 52; 47:31 (?); Exod. 4:31; Judg. 7:15.

14. B. Jacob, "Beitrage zu einer Einl. in die Ps.," *ZAW* 17, pp. 263-279. P. 276, "Finally it is very questionable whether *tōdāh* ever means thanks, but rather it always means praise, recognition, confession." According to Jacob, a proof for this is to be seen in that Modern Hebrew felt required to form a special word for "thanks": הודיה or הודאה. So also Quell, *op. cit.*, p. 94, note 3: "There is no proof that in the Old Testament *tōdāh* meant thanks; cf. LXX αἴνεσις."

in a sentence in which the one being praised is the subject, "thou hast done," or "thou art . . ."[15]

What was it that led to this differentiation of thanks from praise? Thanking presupposes that the community is no longer primary and no longer self-evident. It presupposes that the community is no longer prior to the individual. The differentiation of thanks from praise presupposes a certain development of individualism. In the giving and receiving of thanks, the man who has become an individual must continually be assured of community. It would therefore be foolish, on the basis of the late differentiation of thanks or of the fact that there is no single word for it in the O.T., to draw the conclusion that in our dealings with one another we might replace thanks by praise. A change, however, takes place in our evaluation of things when it becomes clear that in its essence thanking is something secondary, one way of praising. What makes this word so valuable to modern man is just that element in which it differs from praise or goes beyond it. We speak of "thankfulness," and this is the main thing. Spoken thanks is only an "externality," the expression of the feeling of thankfulness. The important thing is the thankful attitude. All this cannot be expressed by the vocabulary for praise. Surely the main difference lies here. The thankful attitude has its origin in a gift or in a helping or saving deed which someone does for me. It can then be expressed in a great variety of ways, by a word, or by a deed, but the decisive factor is the permanence of the thankful attitude. In primitive thought it is otherwise. For us thankfulness stands in a line; for the primitive man only the first and last points of this line are of interest. Both of these appear more sharply in primitive thought. That is, the beginning and end of what we

15. This distinction between "thanks" and "praise" and the relation of the two words to one another has received very little attention in research. Reference may be made to the work of Frants Buhl, "Über Dankbarkeit im A.T. und die sprachlichen Ausdrücke dafür," *Baudissin-Festschrift*, Giessen, 1918, pp. 71-82. Here our concept of thanks was the starting point; it was assumed without reservation for the O.T. and passages were cited for reference. The same uncritical attitude toward the concept is seen in a statement of Mowinckel (*Ps. Studien*, II, p. 143), "Deepened and spiritualized, humble thankfulness becomes worship."

call thankfulness are contained in the vow and the performance of the vow.[16]

This occurs from time to time in a relationship; thankfulness, the line between these two points, is something that I have, or that I have in me; it is something that I possess as a feeling or as an attitude. For primitive man an attitude does not exist except in its expression, for man does not exist "in himself," but only in community with other men (the Hebrew 'ādām means "mankind"). The same holds true for the relationship of man and God. Modern individualistic thought has interpreted the rejection by the prophets and many of the Psalms of specific cultic acts as meaning that it is not a matter of outward works, but of the "attitude of the heart." This interpretation does not have any basis in either the prophets or the Psalms. In the place of sacrifice the Psalms placed praise and obedience, not an attitude, but activity directed toward God. In relation to God, the concept of thankfulness and that of giving thanks are liable to be misunderstood when they are divorced from the concept of praise. The vocabulary of praise never expresses anything like an attitude or a feeling of gratitude. Where a worshiper in the Psalms says, "I will praise the Lord . . . ," he does not mean, "I will be thankful to God," but, "I will respond to him for what he has done for me."[17]

It comes to this, that in the vocabulary of thanks man remains subject, while in the sentences of praise God is subject: "Thou hast done . . . thou art . . . God is . . ."

Thus today when we translate Psalm 118:1 as "O give thanks to the LORD, for he is good; his steadfast love endures for ever!" this sentence must of necessity be understood in a false manner. An uninstructed member of the congregation can scarely understand this in any other sense than that because God is good, and his steadfast love endures for ever, we are called upon to

16. This is the reason why the vow at the end of a petition is an essential, inseparable part of the prayer. This is so not only in the O.T., but also in Babylon and in primitive prayers, while in our prayers it is wholly or almost wholly absent.
17. Wendel, op. cit., p. 172: "Thanks as a thankful attitude that is not expressed is unknown to the O.T."

thank him. That is, (a) we should be grateful to him, (b) we should express our thanks for what God has given us: "I thank thee, O God, that thou . . ." This is not what is meant. Where is there to be found in the entire Psalter a prayer of thanks with this type of structure? What there is in the Psalter, how-ever, seems at first to be a minimum, but it strikes deep. With this *hōdū* we are not called to a sentence in which *I* am the sub-ject, but to one in which *God* is subject. There is such a sentence in the same Psalm a few lines later in verse 5. This difference, that in the thanks of the Psalter God is always the subject, but in our thanks almost always "I" or "we" is the subject, can scarcely be overestimated.

The third factor is that all the vocabulary of praise contains a forensic element. This is particularly expressed in the vow of praise, "I will tell of thy name to my brethren; in the midst of the congregation I will praise thee" (Ps. 22:22). That is what we are called on to do in Ps. 118:1. This is a further reason why the translation "give thanks" is false here, for today no one considers this element to be a part of giving thanks. How dif-ferent it would be, if everywhere, where in our translations of the Psalms we are called on to give thanks, the forensic element were also heard. Then it would be clear that this call, "give thanks . . . ," has been truly heard only by the one, who in addi-tion to having a deep feeling of gratitude in his heart and to thanking God in private, also tells *in public* what God has done for him.

SUMMARY AND CONCLUSIONS

We began with the question, What is a hymn?, and then considered the three possible answers. We have seen from this that it cannot be completely comprehended under any of the three main concepts. It is only secondarily a literary unit, and for the most ancient and very short hymns the concept of a literary unit is not at all appropriate. On the other hand it cannot simply be said that it is cultic, that its Sitz-im-Leben is the service of worship, even though this is certainly true of the great hymns of the postexilic era, for example, Ps. 136. Certainly the Song of Miriam cannot be so described. The general concept "prayer" fits best that which occurs in a hymn, but the caution must be made that our modern concept of prayer cannot be simply applied to the content of those passages in the Psalms. This is conditioned above all by the fact that in the Psalms, as in the O.T. generally, giving thanks is surrounded by praise, is contained within praise, that therefore instead of our contrast of thanks and petition, there stands in the Psalms the contrast of praise and lament (supplication).

It will be then necessary to replace the designations "hymn" and "song of thanks" with other terms for the categories of the Psalms. In view of the present status of Psalm research this demand must be made unconditionally, for it exists quite apart from the results and proposals of this present work. Both these concepts are inadequate. I do not believe it is possible to avoid recognizing this. "Hymn" is determined by form, "song of thanks" (or Psalm of thanks) by content. Hymn is a literary (or cultic) designation; giving thanks is a means of prayer. The designations of the categories as such would not be so important if certain preconceptions were not already contained in them. The inadequacy of the designations of the categories has been an important contributing factor to the failure to let the appropriate categories and their relationship to each other be seen clearly.

Since the essential occurrence in both of these groups of Psalms is the praise of God, I propose to call them both Psalms of praise. The difference between the two groups lies in the fact that the so-called hymn praises God for his actions and his being as a whole (descriptive praise), while the so-called song of thanks praises God for a specific deed, which the one who has been delivered recounts or reports in his song (declarative praise; it could also be called confessional praise).

The term "declarative praise" is simply a reproduction of that which actually lies before us in this group of Psalms. Gunkel too saw this, although he retained the traditional terminology:

". . . the song of thanks of Israel, like the song of thanks of the individual, was originally a report of God's help" *(Einleitung,* p. 318). Declarative praise corresponds to the Hebrew verb *hōdāh.*[18]

The other mode of praise, descriptive praise, corresponds to the Hebrew *hillēl.* It does not praise a unique act of God that has just occurred, but summarizes his activity in its fullness and praises God in the totality of his dealings with men and of his being. It does not have, like declarative praise, a specific, unique occasion; it is not a confession of the one saved, but it looks at the "mighty God's great deeds" in all times and in all places and praises him for them all. This designation is also derived from the actual content of this group of Psalms.[19, 20]

18. Cf. H. Grimme, "Der Begriff von hebräischem hōdāh und tōdāh," *ZAW* 58, 1940/1941, pp. 234-240. "The basic meaning is confess; this is to be divided as follows:
(a) confess, i.e., recognize.
(b) confess, i.e., declare, make known."
(That these two meanings originally belonged together is shown by Horst in relation to Josh. 7, "Die Doxologien im Amosbuch," *ZAW* 47, 1929, pp. 45-54: "Doxology and confession thus belong here of necessity to the public, legal act." See also Wendel, *Laiengebet,* p. 164.)
I agree with Grimme's main thesis: the basic meaning of *hōdāh* is to confess, to affirm. Still, it does not seem to correspond to the vocabulary of the O.T. to say with Grimme that in relation to God, confession is primarily a "confession of the existence of Yahweh," to which is added then a "confession of his principle attributes" (can one confess attributes?). A further development would then be the citing of individual passages where these attributes are mentioned (p. 236). In my opinion it can be clearly proven that confession originally had as its object an act of God, just as the confession of sin (Josh. 7 or Ps. 32:5) had as its object an act of man. The strongest proof of this is the fact that *hōdāh* as used in the Psalms originally belonged to declarative praise, not to descriptive. When Grimme himself equates this "confess" with "proclaim" he thereby indirectly confirms what has been said here. In any case proclamation always has as its primary object an occurrence, an event; not, however, being or attributes, which can be called events only when accurate usage has decayed. A later reference of Grimme's is, however, to be noted, in which he says, pp. 239 f., that *hōdāh* often stands in the O.T. in places later taken over by the concept of faith.
19. The distinction between declarative and descriptive praise is seen also outside the Psalter in the Israelite personal names. (Cf. the work of Martin Noth, *Die israelitischen Personennamen,* Stuttgart, 1928.) In the names that express praise the two groups are clearly distinguished: names which report an act of God (or confess an act of God), such as Elnathan, Jochanan, and names which describe God, such as Abram, Tobijah, Achihud. Declarative praise is much more common in names. A more thorough comparison between the praise of God (and the confession of confidence) in names and in the Psalms is needed. As far as I know, there is no motif from the Psalms that is not reflected in personal names also.
20. This distinction between declarative (or confessional) and descriptive praise is also of significance for the history of Christian hymnology. It is not accidental that Luther's songs have for the most part the character of confessional praise. The hymn of the Reformation, "Nun freut euch . . ." ["Dear Christians one and all

In order to see the total picture, let us look at the changes that would result in the categories of the Psalms. All "thou-Psalms," that is, all that speak to God in the second or third person, are governed by the polarity of petition and praise. These are further divided into Psalms of praise and Psalms of petition.

The Psalms of petition may be divided according to subject as follows:

Lament or petition of the people. (LP)
Lament or petition of the individual. (LI)

Here an observation is necessary concerning "petition." Since in the place of our contrast of petition and thanks there is in the Psalms another, that of petition and praise, "petition" must then be understood somewhat differently from our present concept. It would be more accurate to designate the contrast as that of supplication and praise. In "petition" two elements are present which are clearly distinguished in Hebrew: (a) The (transitive) petition for something (*šā'al*). This petition voices specific requests. A prayer of petition (tautology!) is generally understood as the listing of various requests. There is nothing like this in the Psalms. Occasionally a single request for something (e.g., intercession for the king) is added to a Psalm. There is never a prayer of petition that summarizes various requests: (b) Supplication in time of need (intransitive) is something entirely different (Hebrew *hithpallēl*).[21] This supplication does not have an object like that of a petition, but is always supplication for salvation. The "object" of supplication is determined by the situation of the suppliant. We might also say that the

---

rejoice . . ."] corresponds to the structure of the declarative Psalm of praise. (See below, p. 110.) Moreover his Christmas hymn, "Vom Himmel hoch . . ." ["From Heaven Above to Earth I Come"] is declarative praise. On the other hand, the hymns of the Enlightenment, insofar as they are praise of God, are almost entirely descriptive praise, usually very reflective, nearer to the Psalms of the Apocrypha than to those of the Psalter; e.g., "Wenn ich, o Schöpfer, deine Macht . . ." (Gellert). The descriptive songs of praise of the Middle Ages, however, are much nearer the canonical Psalms, as for instance the song of Meissner, "Gott ist gewaltig, vielgestaltig . . ." (musical setting of Albert Becker, "Ein neues Lied").

21. The word originally meant "to make intercession."

"object" of this supplication is the lament. Thus lamentation is a necessary part of this supplication. It is not every request for something, but this supplication in time of need, that is the opposite pole of praise.

Thus in the interest of accuracy one should always say "supplication" instead of "petition" in the Psalms. Since, however, our word "petition" includes both concepts it would be very difficult to displace entirely the terms "petition" and "Psalm of petition."* They will therefore be retained with the reservation expressed here. From this point of view the designation "Psalm of lament," which has gained general acceptance in O.T. studies, has a certain justification. The petition which is meant here receives its distinctive character from the lament. Even though the core of all these Psalms, their σκόπος, is not lament but petition (or supplication), the justification of the customary designation "Psalm of lament" cannot be disputed. I shall follow this designation in the abbreviations which I use in this work.

The petitions of the individual constitute by far the largest category in the Psalter. Here however a further classification is necessary; for a large number of petitionary Psalms this designation is no longer accurate, for they are not *merely* lament and petition but petition that has been *heard*. At the end of these heard petitions there is a part that breaks over into declarative praise.

The *Psalms of praise* fall into two groups on the basis of the two different modes of praise (see above p. 31):

Declarative praise (God has acted);
Descriptive praise (God is ... does) (P).

Of these, only the declarative Psalms of praise may be distinguished by categories:

The declarative Psalm of praise of the people (PP);
The declarative Psalm of praise of the individual (PI).

---

* Translator's note: "Petition" as a noun and as a verb has been adopted as the translation of the German "Bitte" and "bitten," and "supplication," etc., for the German "Flehen." Although these terms do not reproduce all the connotations of the German original they seem to be more adequate than any others.

In the descriptive Psalm of praise, the praise of the people (or of the congregation) and the praise of the individual are combined. Only a few of these Psalms can be distinguished by subject, and this distinction cannot be made on the basis of categories.

All the "smaller categories" are not to be placed alongside these two great categories, but are to be included in them or can be derived from them. That is to say, in them a motif from one of the two major categories has become independent. (These smaller categories must be omitted from this discussion.)

In this analysis of the Psalms, "category" is primarily neither a literary nor a cultic concept. It is both of these, but only secondarily. This analysis is determined by the two basic modes of speaking to God: praise and petition.

This basic thesis is not derived from the exegesis of the O.T. Psalms alone, but from the larger environment of which they are a part, and out of the study of which the history and distinctive character of the O.T. Psalms become clear. This can be shown first of all by an investigation of the praise of God in the Babylonian-Assyrian psalms.

PART TWO

The Structure of the Babylonian Psalms

The Babylonian psalms have one essential in common with those of the Bible: they speak to God in terms of petition and praise. In Babylon as in Israel, praising God and supplicating him were an essential part of life.

Basic to the Babylonian psalms is a structure in which five major parts may be recognized:[1]

    I. Address[2]

    II. Praise
(Stummer: "depiction of majesty." Cumming: "ascription of praise.")[3]

    III. Lament[4]

    IV. Petition[5]

    V. Vow of praise[6]

1. This structure was primarily worked out by Stummer, *Sumer.-akkad. Parallelen*, 1922, p. 9. Stummer listed a further element, "self-introduction of the prayer." Subsequently the structure of the Babylonian psalms was further worked out. See especially Falckenstein, "Die Haupttypen der sumer. Gebetsbeschwörung," *LSSt*, NF, 1931, and W. G. Kunstmann, "Die babyl. Gebetsbeschwörung," *LSSt*, NF, 2, 1932, especially p. 7.

2. In reference to the address, cf. Kunstmann's summary, pp. 7 ff., for the category of adjuratory prayers. On p. 68 of the same work there is listed further literature for the investigation of the address to the various gods. Cf. Cumming, *op. cit.*, pp. 56 ff.

3. I have not found a single Babylonian psalm in which praise was entirely lacking (except for fragments). There are however extreme differences in the type and extent of praise. Two extremes are as follows: in a song to Marduk praise consists of only one sentence with two relative clauses (Zimmern A, p. 17): "Mighty Marduk, whose wrath is a deluge, but who is a merciful father to those reconciled to him." On the other hand, the great hymn to Shamash is composed entirely of praise (Zimmern B, 23-27).

4. Pp. 17 ff. For the forms of lament, cf. Kunstmann, *op. cit.*, pp. 17 ff.

5. Examples for the petition: Zimmern A, p. 17; King Mag 27:15 ff., 18; *KM* 27:19 ff.; Z 42; Ż 80; Zimmern A, p. 22 ff.; Zimmern B 4; Ż 19. Address of praise: Z 20, "I have sacrificed to thee," Z 21. Petition: Zimmern B 17, Z 14 ff.; Zimmern B, p. 19. Cf. Kunstmann, *op. cit.*, p. 25 for further examples.

6. Examples are given by Stummer, *op. cit.*, pp. 103 f., and Kunstmann, *op. cit.*, pp. 39-42.

Naturally this structure does not appear in schematic form in each psalm,[7] and there are a great many variations of it. Nevertheless the order of the various parts is almost always preserved.

Even in these five principal parts the Babylonian psalms correspond with those of the O.T.

1. The most significant distinction is that in the Babylonian psalms these five motifs constitute one psalm. In the O.T., on the other hand, these five motifs are divided among two psalm categories. The caesura comes between the second and the third parts. A division of psalms of petition and praise on the basis of categories is unknown in the Babylonian psalms. Praise of God has here a much broader field than it has in the Psalms of the O.T., but it is primarily introductory and at the same time preparatory for petition. The same is true of the Egyptian psalms.

(a) In the Psalms of lament in the O.T. the lament or petition follows directly after the address, and these are never introduced or anticipated by detailed praise (Neh. 1:5 ff.; 2 Macc. 1:24 ff.). The address is almost never expanded by honor-giving predicates such as are encountered in great number in Babylonian psalms (as many as 36 in one psalm[8]).

(b) Address and praise, that is, parts I and II, constitute in the O.T. an independent Psalm category, that of descriptive praise. At the same time, something entirely new has been added to the Psalms of praise of the O.T.: the imperative exhortation to praise. This imperative call to praise is never encountered in the Babylonian psalms.[9]

---

7. Ebeling I, p. 18 to Nabu, *KAR* 1, Nr. 25, 23.
   Ebeling I, p. 19 to Marduk, *KAR* I, Nr. 23.
   Ebeling I, p. 44 to Shamash, K 2132, VAT 8242.
   Ebeling I, pp. 70-72 to ? (fragment), *KAR* III, 129.
   Ebeling II, p. 14 to Tamuz, VAT 8261.
   Ebeling II, pp. 17 f. to Tamuz, VAT 10034.
   Ebeling II, p. 37 to Ishtar (Vows of praise, preserved in fragmentary condition).
8. Cumming, *op. cit.*, p. 61. "It was easy to expand indefinitely the invocation from its natural length of four to six lines until the invocation becomes itself hymnal praise of the god." (Sin 5, invocation 23 lines!). See also Begrich, *op. cit.*, p. 233.
9. This fact is mentioned by Stummer, *op. cit.*, p. 26, and Cumming in the conclusion of his work, *op. cit.*, p. 155.

2. Another difference is closely related to this one. In the Babylonian psalms praise of God is almost exclusively descriptive praise. The being of the god and his actions in general are praised. From this Stummer took his term "description of majesty" (*Herrlichkeitsschilderung*). Praise on the basis of a single act of God (declarative praise) is almost entirely absent.

3. That the god whom this praise exalts is one god among others has quite definite consequences.

(a) The emphasis of praise does not lie on what occurs between God and man, but on what occurs among the gods. (Here praise can even pass into mythical accounts, as, for example, "Flute Lament for Adad," Zimmern B, p. 7, or "Ishtar's Elevation to Queen of Heaven," Gressmann, *Texte,* pp. 252 ff.) One might wonder whether mythical accounts did not develop out of praise of the god.

(b) The one praying must keep in mind not only the god to whom he is praying, but the other gods as well. On the one hand, in his praise he must elevate high above the others the god on whom he calls (thus the often extremely exaggerated language of this praise), and on the other hand he must include them in intercessory petition[10] and praise. The intercession of the saints for which one prays in the Roman church has its exact prototype in the intercession of the other gods, which the suppliant of the Babylonian psalms requests. Especially significant is the fact that the praise of the one praying was to be reinforced by the praise of the other gods. For example, "May my god honor thy might, my goddess proclaim thy greatness" (BMS 12, King).[11] One's own petition and praise needed strengthening through an intermediary. In the matter of conjuring, the tendency goes even further; the gods even need their own (divine) priestly conjurer.[12]

4. The relationship of the Babylonian psalms to those of the O.T. becomes especially clear in the vow of praise. In both in-

---

10. Ebeling I, 7-8: "May the other gods regard him favorably." Ebeling I, 5-6: "Say a good word to Enlil."
11. Conjuration for Shamash, Zimmern 1, p. 15, and Ebeling I, 10-11 for Marduk.
12. Weber, "Dämonenbeschwörungen bei den Babyloniern und Assyrern," p. 7.

stances it is an essential component of prayer.[13] In both it occupies the same position, following the petition (i.e., at the end of the psalm). In form and content the vow of praise in the Babylonian psalms is essentially identical with that of the O.T. For example,

> I will praise and laud thee to the astonishment of later days,
> I will proclaim thy majesty to those who are widely scattered.[14]

In the vow of praise of the Accadian psalms it is quite clear that the opposite pole of petition is not thanks but praise. It is not thanks that is offered but praise, laud, honor, majesty, and service. (Professor Baumgartner has informed me orally that there is in Accadian no differentiated term for "thanks.") As in the Psalms of the O.T., the forensic element is often stressed in those of Babylon. It is a part of praise that others, even many others, hear it.

The vow of praise at the end of the psalm is not merely conclusion. It is more a beginning than a terminus. In it something is promised, something is held in prospect. That which is promised here occurs in Part II, in the ascription of praise.

In the Babylonian psalms there are two developments at the end and at the beginning that say this unambiguously.

(a) In two songs to Ishtar praise follows the vow of praise at the end:

> Among the black-headed ones I will glorify thy deity and thy might.
> Yea, Ishtar is exalted, Ishtar is queen . . . there is none like her . . .

(b) The expansion is more frequently encountered at the beginning. There is a whole group of psalms that begin with clauses that correspond exactly to the vow of praise, but which at the beginning of the psalm can only have the meaning of a

---

13. Stummer, *op. cit.*, p. 102: ". . . in the Babylonian psalms very frequent, almost regular."
14. K ALL 1 and K 6475.

declaration.[15] It can be shown that these sentences are secondary matter in the introduction. Once an introduction which announces praise of God is followed directly by lament and petition. This introduction then became a stereotyped formula.[16]

A song to Ishtar:

> ... my Princess, above and below
> Thy goodness (?) will I proclaim,
> The splendid Ishtar, in her will I exult,
> Princess, elevated to heaven,
> Ishtar, thou art great!
> Lady Ishtar, thee will I honor,
> Princess, elevated to heaven,
> Goddess ... thou art great.

These two expansions do not introduce any new motif or add any new part. In one case Part II is added to Part V (the beginning to the conclusion), and in the other Part V has been moved to the beginning. Here it can be seen that the sequence of the five motifs is a circle, that is, that Part V is open toward Parts I and II. The vow of praise is to some extent the link between the two main parts, between the lament and petition on the one hand and the praise to god on the other. The vow of praise promises to the god, to whom the suppliant cries out in his need, the praise of his name.

Here a comparison with the Psalms of the O.T. shows that the above-mentioned two main differences between the psalms of Babylon and those of Israel (I. Babylon, *one* main category, praise and petition; Israel, *two* main categories, Psalm of praise and Psalm of petition. II. Babylon, almost only descriptive praise; Israel, declarative and descriptive praise) have the same root. In the Psalms of Israel we often find the two expansions that have been indicated in the Babylonian psalms.

(a) The expansion at the end. In a large number of LI the vow of praise at the end of the Psalm is followed by yet additional praise of God.

15. K 3258, Zimmern B, p. 20, Gressmann, *op. cit.,* p. 267.
16. Gressmann, *op. cit.,* p. 267.

Ps. 13:6: "I will sing to the LORD, because he has dealt bountifully with me."

Ps. 54:7: "For thou hast delivered me from every trouble . . ." Cf. also 51:11 f.; 71:24; 69:33, etc.

When these clauses are compared with the expansions in the two songs of Ishtar, the difference is obvious; there descriptive praise, here declarative praise

(b) The expansion at the beginning. In exact correspondence to the way the Babylonian psalms begin in verbal agreement with the vow of praise at the end, but with the sense of a proclamation at the beginning, a great many of the Psalms of the O.T. begin with the proclamation, "I will praise . . ." or a similar expression. This proclamation, however, never introduces a descriptive Psalm of praise but always a declarative Psalm of praise. (In late extra-canonical psalms this proclamation is also found in descriptive Psalms of praise.)

This means therefore that the circle of five motifs in one psalm was possible in Babylon because the vow of praise is intended to be descriptive praise (at the end) and introduces it (at the beginning). Thereby the praise of God for a specific, unique deed, which is begun at this place in the Psalms of the O.T., is bypassed. A remnant of declarative praise can often be found in the appositional phrases of the address (e.g., "who hears prayer").[17]

In some instances the address is expanded by so many appositional expressions that it becomes itself a psalm of praise. (See Cumming, op. cit., p. 61. The address can be as long as 23 lines!) The declarative psalm of praise presupposes a lapse of time between the supplication in dire need and the reporting of the marvelous help of God that has been experienced. If praise, as in most of the Babylonian psalms, precedes lament and petition

17. Further examples are as follows:
"Who destroy evil" (KM 62, 9. Ea, Marduk, Shamash 1a).
"Who bring deliverance" (KM 62, 9. Ea, Marduk, Shamash 1a).
"Who cut the thread of misfortune" (Marduk, Shamash 1a).
"Who causes her words to be heard" (Tasmetu 2, KM 33, 2).
"Who frees the captives" (Nergal 1, KM 287).
"Who intercedes" (Gula 1, Sarpanitum 1, KM 6, 90; 9, 45).
"Who hears prayer" (Shamash 35, KM 59, 5).

it can only be a general, timeless, descriptive praise. This is the basis of the fact that in Babylon declarative praise is so insignificant in comparison with the descriptive that it almost vanishes entirely.

In this way the real difference in the manner of speaking to God in these two settings now becomes completely clear. In both cultures the one praying stands within the circle of petition and praise; in both the turning point is the vow of praise, which leads from petition into praise. The difference lies in the fact that in the Babylonian psalm the emphasis lies entirely on the praise which prepares the way for the petition, and in the Psalms of the O.T. it lies entirely on the praise that looks back on the wonderful help of God in intervening.

In Babylon the psalms primarily praise the one who exists, the god who exists in his world of gods. In Israel they primarily praise the God who acts marvelously by intervening in the history of his people and in the history of the individual member of his people. The gods praised in Babylon have their history among the gods. In Israel's praise from beginning to end the basic theme is the history of God with his people.

Literature on the Babylonian Psalms

Begrich: "Die Vertrauensäusserungen im israelitischen Klagelied des Einzelnen und in seinen babylonischen Gegenstücken," *ZAW* 46, 1928.

Cumming, C. G.: *The Assyrian and Hebrew Hymns of Praise,* 1934.

Driver: *The Psalms in the Light of Babylonian Research.*

Blackmann: "The Psalms in the Light of Egyptian Research" (in Simpson: *The Psalmists*), Oxford, 1926.

Ebeling, E.: *Quellen zur Kenntnis der babylonischen Religion,* 1918.

Ebeling, E.: *Babylonisch-assyrische Texte,* 1933.

Gressmann, H.: *Altorientalische Texte und Bilder zum A.T.,* 1926/27.

Falckenstein, S.: "Die Haupttypen der sumerischen Gebetsbeschwörung," *LSSt,* NF 2, 1931.

Böllenrücher, J.: *Gebete und Hymnen an Nergal,* Leipzig, 1904.

Hehn, J.: *Hymnen und Gebete an Marduk,* Leipzig, 1905.

Kunstmann, W. G.: "Die babylonische Gebetsbeschwörung," *LSSt,* NF 2, 1932.

Stummer, Fr.: *Sumerisch-akkadische Parallelen zum Aufbau alttestamentlicher Psalmen,* Paderborn, 1922.

Weber, O.: "Dämonenbeschwörungen bei den Babyloniern und Assyrern," *Der Alte Orient* VII, 4.

Zimmern, H.: "Babylonische Hymnen und Gebete," *Der Alte Orient*
VII, 3 und XIII, 1, 1905 and 1911.

Bahr, H.: *Die babylonischen Busspsalmen und das A.T.*, Leipzig, 1918.

Widengren, G.: *The Accadian and Hebrew Psalms of Lamentation as
Religious Documents,* 1937 (not available to me before completion
of this work).

Jastrow, M.: *Die Religion Babyloniens und Assyriens,* 3 vols., Giessen,
1905-12.

EXCURSUS: THE PRAISE OF GOD IN THE EGYPTIAN PSALMS

I have taken as my sources here A. Erman, *Die Literatur der
alten Ägypter,* Leipzig, 1923, and G. Roeder, *Urkunden zur
Religion des alten Ägypten,* Jena, 1915, and in addition, A. M.
Blackman, "The Psalms in the Light of Egyptian Research,"
in Simpson, *The Psalmists,* 1926, and Gressmann, *AOT.*

It will not be possible here to give a comprehensive presentation, but the most important similarities and differences will be
pointed out.

The most striking difference between the Egyptian and the
Babylonian psalms lies in the astonishing predominance of
praise and confidence in those of Egypt. The call to rejoice,
but even more the depicting of joy, jubilation, and praise occupy a significant place, while they are rarely encountered in
the Babylonian psalms. In correspondence to this there is on
the other hand very little of the deep anxiety that stands behind
a major part of the Babylonian psalms.

Although similarities and points of contact are present, the
differences are the expression of different basic attitudes toward
the gods.

When the Egyptian psalms speak to the gods there is a preponderance of self-confident assurance, which pushes lament and
supplication into the background in favor of a contemplative
or pictorial narration that rejoices in the splendor and beauty
of the gods. This great self-assurance is striking. In a very
detailed self-justification of the dead before the judge of the
dead we read (Roeder, *op. cit.,* pp. 274 ff.): "Lo, I come to thee,

filled with righteousness . . ." It is seen also in that we never
encounter the expressions so frequent in the Babylonian psalms,
"whom I know—do not know," but very often encounter the
assurance, "I know him," "I know thee." In the journeys of the
dead the knowledge of names plays an important role.

We very seldom encounter laments. In Erman's work there
is a detailed lament only in the prayer to Amon, p. 381, over
a "year of misery." But this too is more objective description
than a true cry of dire need. The distinction of the prayers of
the poor from all others is particularly striking. (See Roeder,
op. cit., pp. 52-58 f., "Memorials of the Poor.") It is almost only
here that we meet true confession of sin, and genuine, strong
lamentation. The speaking to God is here much more immediate. The mythical-cultic element almost disappears. Especial
reference should be made to the "Prayer of the Penitent Sinner"
(Roeder, *op. cit.,* p. 57). Also, Erman, *op. cit.,* p. 380, the lament
of a poor man from whom the court demands too much. Both
laments, however, occur in prayers which resemble the "heard
petitions" of the Psalter. The first is quite certain of being heard,
and the major part of the second prayer consists of praise and
expressions of confidence. In both the transition is easily recognized. Both times it is introduced, "There one finds, that
Amon . . ."

The same feature is noticeable in the prayer of Neb-re, painter
in the service of Amon (Erman, *op. cit.,* pp. 383 f. and Gunkel,
Einleitung, pp. 287 f.). The structure closely approaches that of
the declarative praise of the Psalms. After an introductory summary we read as follows:

> He wrote hymns to his name,
> For his might is so great,
> And wrote laments before him,
> Before the whole land,
> For the sake of Nacht-Amon the painter,
> Who was sick and near death,
> Who had incurred the wrath of Amon
> Because of his cow (?).

At the point where the report of his plight has its proper place, the one praying steps out of his prayer and reports only that during the illness of his son he wrote songs of praise and of lament (or petition?). The one praying is thus not the one who is sick or who has been healed. We find here the sentence so frequent in the psalms, "Thou Amon art he who rescues the one who is in the world of the dead." However, this does not come in the report, but in the introductory confession of confidence. Thus here the reality of the plight has moved in a remarkable way into the background. An immediate, loud, distraught cry to God is nowhere to be found.

This agrees with the observation made concerning the petitions. Petitions for salvation out of a presently threatening need are inconspicuous. There is one petition for a just judgment (p. 379): "Amon, incline thine ear to one who stands alone in judgment, to one who is poor, but whose foe is wealthy." And once, "Come to me, save me in this year of misery!" There is one prayer of confession, p. 379, that sounds, however, more like mere excuses.

The majority of the petitions are for something constant, something which does not arise from acute need:

"That thou wouldest care for me," p. 379.
"That thou wouldest grant me skill in my office," p. 377.
"Send me to Hermopolis, where one can live in comfort!", p. 377.
Petition for the promotion of the teacher, p. 379.

In all these petitions lament is naturally missing. Especially typical is the prayer to Thoth, p. 377, which begins with the petition for transfer to Hermopolis. In the middle of the text these words appear: "Come, save me." This petition for salvation has already become quite stereotyped and can be spoken where there is no question of salvation in the strict sense.

It is quite clear that the petition for salvation was originally in two parts, (a) come to me! and (b) save me! So also pp. 381, 379, 377 (only in the middle of the song).

The confession of confidence and the certainty of being heard are encountered frequently and are expressed forcefully, pp. 377, 379. "Come to me, Re Harakhte . . . ," pp. 380, 381, 383. But it has already been pointed out that this point must not be seen in isolation. The counterbalance to these words of confidence and the certainty of a hearing, *the vow of praise,* is absent. Little can be seen here of the strict way in which in the Babylonian psalms the vow of praise must of necessity follow the petition. Only once does it clearly stand at the end of a petition, but it is there in the form of a petition (p. 377): "Come to me and care for me, I am indeed . . . Let me speak of thy mighty deeds, in whatever land I am; then the people will say, What God does is great. . . ."

In the prayer to Amon, p. 381, it is merely hinted at. There is, however, a clear and detailed witness to it in the memorial of the painter Neb-re, pp. 383 f., and it is by this that we learn of the vow of praise as a fixed form. This makes all the more notable the fact that it is usually missing in prayers.

Praise

1. The relation of praise and petition to each other: In the Babylonian psalms, it is almost always the rule that praise precedes and prepares the way for petition. The same thing is found in the Egyptian psalms, where, while it is not so regular, it still predominates. Thus it is in all three songs to the crowns on p. 35 (even though the relationship of petition to praise is different in each of the three songs). In addition, pp. 184, 185?, 186, 362, 374, 375 (in Songs to the Sun and to Osiris), 379 (in prayers of petition to Re and in prayers to Amon), 381 (in the song to Amon the petition is in the form of an expression of confidence). Two extremes can be seen. In the songs to the morning sun, p. 184, the petition is merely appended at the conclusion, and it is quite indefinite: "Illumine me that I may see thy beauty!" The emphasis is entirely on praise. The song to the sun god, p. 374, is just the opposite. Here the powerful praise of the sun god very clearly has the significance of

preparing for very concrete petitions. "Give thou it (my office) to me again! Lo, I see another occupy it." Here the Egyptian psalm agrees with the Babylonian as over against the biblical. Nowhere in the O.T. is the praise of God used in this manner as the means to an end. A distinction to the Babylonian psalms is that often a word of praise follows the petition (e.g., p. 36, the three songs to the crown, and p. 377, prayer to Thoth).

2. There is, however, a large group of psalms that consist only of an address of praise—praise and the depiction of majesty (Cumming: ascription of praise).

(a) Most of these songs are reminiscent of the epiphany psalms. An actual epiphany is found in the song, pp. 30-32, "The Dead Man Devours the Gods." The appearance of god, its consequences, and its effect are described. The expression here, ". . . when they see him, as he appears," corresponds to the Babylonian "when thou comest forth." The motif is taken up once again at the end, "He it is that rises and rises . . ." In between, the song contains only praise and ascriptions of praise, such as, "His majesty is in heaven, his might is on the horizon," and "He it is who devours men and lives on gods."

Likewise the second crown song, p. 35. "Praise to thee, thou eye of Horus . . . when thou arisest in the Eastern horizon"; p. 183 to Min-Horus, "Praise to thee, Min, in thine appearing . . ."; p. 184 to the morning sun, "Praise to thee who now arisest, and who illuminest the two lands when thou comest forth"; p. 185, to the evening sun, "Praise to thee, when thou goest down, Atum, Harakhte. . . ."

In addition, see also the songs on pp. 187-192, 354, 357, 362, 374, 375.

Now, however, an important change becomes noticeable within these epiphany songs, which must be followed through in a wider area. The early epiphany formula ran, "When thou arisest," "When he appears." Later this form changes to a simple description in a relative clause, e.g., p. 357, the fourth song of the great hymn to Amon. "Thou only king . . . among the gods . . . who arisest in the Eastern horizon and settest on the Western

horizon . . . ," or in a main clause, p. 362, a prayer for the king
in Tel-Amarna, "Thou arisest in beauty, thou ascendest the
horizon of heaven to bring life to all that thou hast made . . . ,"
and p. 374, to the sun god, "Thou awakest in beauty, thou Horus,
who journiest over the heaven."

Here a tendency becomes clear which attracts attention in the
comparison of all the Egyptian psalms of praise to those of
Babylon, and even more in comparison to the Hebrew. This is
quite clearly the descriptive praise of an onlooker.

In addition there is a type of praise that clearly passes into
mythical tales: pp. 187-192, a song of praise for Osiris, and pp.
363-373, the "1000 Songs," poems to Thebes and its god. This
type is found frequently in the Babylonian psalms.

The other type, however, predominates, that of describing
what is observed: p. 375, "Thou splendid and bright . . . thou
beautiful sun with glowing light . . . and how mysterious is he
. . . thou splendid sun with white light"; p. 374, "Thou awakest
in beauty . . . thou child of flame with sparkling beams"; p. 184,
"Enlighten me, that I may see thy beauty!"; p. 185, "Thou art
beautiful, O Re, all the days!"; p. 186, ". . . how he shines in his
crown! . . ."; pp. 193-196, "Thou makest green, thou makest
green, O Nile, thou makest green!"; p. 354, "Thy beauty con-
quers hearts . . ."; p. 357, "The gods shout for joy at thy
beauty . . ."; p. 362, "He shouts for joy when he sees thy beauty."
This tendency finds even stronger expression in that a depiction of praise is almost always added to this depiction of glory.

There is also a call to praise, and many songs begin, "Praise
to thee!" This corresponds approximately to the Hebrew *bārūk!*
In the Babylonian there is nothing to correspond to this. Examples are: p. 35, second and third crown song, pp. 183, 184, 185,
187, 192, 193, 352, 353, 354 (here also at the end in accordance
with the practice of forming a framework), and 378.

This "Praise to thee!" is thus an introductory call to praise in
the same place where in the Hebrew descriptive Psalms of praise
the call to praise stands in the imperative. Even in the Egyptian
there is occasionally an imperative. For example, p. 186, ad-

dressed to the gods: "O ye gods, come and see . . . how splendid he is in his crown . . . Shout for joy . . . Honor him, magnify him, offer him praise!"

It may also be addressed to men. At the end of the song of praise to the Nile, pp. 193-196: "All ye men, exalt the nine gods and be in awe . . ." Also at the beginning of the declarative psalm of praise of the painter Neb-re, p. 383: "Let sons and daughters tell it, great and small; tell it generation after generation, those who have not yet arisen, tell it to the fish in the water and the birds . . . tell it to him who knows it and to him who knows it not. Beware of him!" Only the introduction, "Praise to thee!", had become a fixed form, but alongside it the depicting of praise had taken a large place. Corresponding to the change in the epiphany formula there is probably here an earlier form in which honoring and shouting for joy (especially of the gods, then of the creation, then of men) were a result of the epiphany. The first effect of the epiphany is fear and trembling. On p. 30: ". . . the bones of the earth god tremble . . . when they see him as he appears . . ." Compare above, "Beware of him!" But this is rare. For the most part only jubilation and praise are depicted. On p. 35, in the second crown song: ". . . over whose beauty the nine gods shout for joy, when he arises in the Eastern horizon." Later the shouting for joy, the praise, the rejoicing, were only described. This depicting of the honoring and the rejoicing at the appearance of the gods or over their deeds, such as victory, creation, preservation, is almost never lacking. On p. 184, the song to the morning sun reads: "All the Nine praise thee . . . all mankind rejoices in him, the souls of Heliopolis rejoice in him, the buffoons honor him. Praise to thee! all that is wild cries together."

Further depictions of praise are found on pp. 185-186. In the song of praise to Osiris the introductory praise is so permeated with the depiction of praise that they occur in alternate lines, but the depiction of praise outweighs actual praise. On p. 192, song of praise for Osiris, the motif is expanded remarkably, "Thousands praise thee." The number becomes important!

In several places, e.g., p. 354, the third song to Amon, it is quite clear how gradually in the depiction of praise, love takes the place of praise. "Love for thee is spread through the two lands." "Thou art loved in the southern heaven and lovely in the northern heaven." Page 356: "Beloved in Karnak . . ." Page 357: "Praise to thee, Amon Re, from Karnak, whose rising is beloved by his city." This song too is full of depiction of praise and love. Likewise the Song IV, p. 374, to the sun god. Here we encounter a profound difference from the O.T.: the dead praise god! "Those who sleep all praise together thy beauty, when thy light shines before their face . . ." It corresponds to the tone of these psalms, in which the bright side of being stands so much in the foreground, that the other side—death, anxiety, evil powers, doubt—has almost disappeared.

The elevated meaning and wide distribution of the depictions of praise is characteristic of the Egyptian psalms. In the Babylonian psalms it is also encountered, but not so often and not so widespread, and it is usually strictly an effect of the epiphany. The contrast to the Psalms of the O.T. is much sharper here. In them the depiction of praise is encountered only seldom, and only in late Psalms. While the vocabulary of praise in the Egyptian psalms is overwhelmingly indicative, and thus depicts, that of the O.T. in all its fullness is almost only imperative. In the Egyptian psalms the laud and praise of the gods is constantly described as occurring in a contemplative attitude. In the Psalms of the O.T. we have almost always calls to praise. There it is a fact, but here a demand; there it is something given to God, but here something owed to God; there God is the one who receives and has received the praise, while in Israel God is the one whose deeds are an ever new call to praise.

In the praise of God in the Egyptian psalms taken as a whole, a contemplative attitude is prevalent. There is also some declarative praise, but it occurs very seldom. Descriptive praise here is not, like that of the Old Testament, the development of the concept of the majesty and goodness of God, nor is it to the same degree as in the psalms of Babylon a listing of predicates and clauses of praise. In Egypt descriptive praise had before it as in a picture the god, his appearance, his history, and it was then his beauty that was praised. In this praise it is not so much a question of God's being for us as it is of God's being for himself in his world of gods and in his own history.

PART THREE

The Praise of God
in the Categories of the Psalms

THE PSALM OF PETITION OR LAMENT OF THE PEOPLE (LP)

The structure is as follows:

I. Address
   Introductory Petition
II. Lament
III. Confession of Trust
IV. Petition (Double Wish)[1]
V. Vow of Praise

These five elements are basic to the structure of the lament of the people. The introductory petition is not an essential part, but it is encountered precisely in the early Psalms and most probably belonged to the original structure of this category of Psalm. The double wish is rare. It probably belongs properly to the lament of the individual and was secondarily included in the lament of the people. The following expansions were likely late:

At the beginning: praise of God by way of introduction.

In the middle: after the petition an expression of the certainty of being heard, and expansions of a reflective nature.

At the end: concluding petition or praise of God.

---

1. That is, a wish or a petition that simultaneously is expressed in two directions. May God do thus to our enemies; may God do thus to us. An example is found in Ps. 80:17-18. Cf. the table.

Structure of the Laments of the People

		79	74	80
Address and introductory cry for help		O God	O God / Why? / Remember / Direct thy steps	Give ear, O Shepherd of Israel
Reference to God's earlier saving deeds		(thy inheritance)	Remember thy congregation which thou hast gotten . . . redeemed . . . where thou hast dwelt	thou who leadest Joseph like a flock
Lament	the foes	the heathen have come into thy inheritance	The foes have roared in the midst of thy holy place	our enemies laugh all . . . feed on it
	we	We have become a taunt to our neighbors	We do not see . . . no longer any prophet None . . . who knows	Thou dost make us the scorn of our neighbors
	thou	How long, O LORD? Wilt thou be angry forever?	why dost thou cast us off forever? How long?	Thou hast fed them with the bread of tears how long?

		we thy people, the flock of thy pasture	Yet God is my King from of old thou hast....	Thou didst bring a vine out of Egypt
Confession of Trust				
Petition	hear!	Do not remember against us / let thy compassion come	Do not forget	Turn again / Look down from heaven
	save!	Help us / deliver us	Do not deliver / Arise	have regard for this vine / Restore us
	punish!	Pour out thy anger / Let the avenging ... be known	Do not forget the clamor of thy foes	——
Motifs		Why should the nations say / the groans of the prisoners / we are brought very low	Is the enemy to revile thy name? / the life of thy poor, thy covenant	The stock which thy right hand planted
Double wish		12-13	——	17-18
Vows of Praise		we ... will give thanks to thee for ever ... / we will recount thy praise	let the poor and needy praise thy name	give us life, and we will call on thy name

There are also some variations in structure:

1. The most constant of all parts is the petition. It is never missing.

2. A tendency for the petition to expand and for the lament to disappear, or to have something substituted for it, is distinctly noticeable. The end result of this tendency can be for the whole Psalm to become petition.

3. In late Psalms direct praise of God often takes the place of the vow of praise.

4. In some Psalms the confession of trust (or the assurance of a hearing) is so dominant that it is possible to speak of a "Psalm of trust for the people." Examples are Pss. 123; 126; The Song of Zion, Ps. 46; perhaps Ps. 90; Ps. Sol. 7.

What is the relationship of the LP to the praise of God? Three motifs of this type of Psalm are to be kept in mind.

1. *The community which is supplicating God makes reference to his saving deeds in the past.* For the most part this occurs at the beginning of the Psalm after the introductory call for help, e.g., Pss. 44:1-3; 85:1-3. These are not really "confessions of trust" although they are very similar, but they are one of the motifs which should move God to intervene. Many of these Psalms are dominated by the tension, "Of old thou hast done thus—and now?"[2]

This act of referring God to his earlier saving deeds takes place in the second person: "Thou hast done . . ." That is the structure of declarative praise. While God is being referred to his earlier saving actions, he is being praised for these actions. Thus in a large group of LP we find declarative praise which serves as one of the motifs which should move God to intervene in the present desperate situation. This is the case in Pss. 44:1-3; 85:1-3; 74:1b-2; 80:8-11; Isa. 63:7-9, 11b-14; Ps. 106:8-11, 43-46. Ps. 83:9-11 might be included here; however, this motif does not form a constituent part of the Psalm but occurs in the petition:

2. The same feature may be seen in prose prayers, e.g., Josh. 7:7-9; Judg. 15:18.

"Do to them as thou didst to Midian, as to Sisera and Jabin . . ."
The same is true of Ecclus. 33:4a.[3]

The significance of this part of the LP is shown quite clearly in Ps. 80 in the figure of the vine:

Vs. 8, "Thou didst bring a vine out of Egypt . . ."
Vs. 12, "Why then hast thou broken down its walls . . . ?"

Ps. 89:19-37 (and 3-4) belongs here also. In this Psalm God's promise to David has taken the place of his saving deeds of old. This portion has undergone an interesting transformation in Ps. 74:13-17, where the summarizing sentence in vs. 12, which speaks of God's saving actions, is expanded in 13-17 by praise of God the creator. God's activity in creation, however, is depicted as entirely analogous to his intervention in history:

Vs. 13, "Thou didst divide the sea by thy might . . ."
This passage has an exact parallel in Isa. 51:9-16, a passage based on an LP.[4]

After the introductory call for help in Isa. 51:9: "Awake, awake, put on strength . . . ," there follows in 9b-10 the reminder:
"Was it not thou that didst cut Rahab in pieces . . .
That didst make the depths of the sea a way . . ."
Here God's creative activity and his saving activity are regarded as identical to such a degree that the one passes into the other without a noticeable break. Thus this passage actually stands in the middle between those passages in which God is reminded of his former saving action and Ps. 74:13-17, where at this place in the structure of the Psalm praise of God the creator is now found.

Both passages, however, show that this portion of the Psalm, which is essentially declarative praise, approaches descriptive praise. To be sure, it is not praise that is called forth by a newly experienced activity of God, but praise that looks back into the

3. Cf. the *Iliad*, I, 451 ff.: "As thou hast heard my former prayer, honored me, and smitten the people of the Achaeans, now also fulfill this wish!" Also, Heiler, *op. cit.*, pp. 89 f.
4. Begrich, *op. cit.*, p. 169. He sees in this an imitation of the LI, "but still with the content of an LP."

distant past, when God—once long ago—did such great things. On this basis it is understandable that in late Psalms descriptive praise is found in the introduction of the LP: Pss. 106:1-3; 89: 5-18 (unless this is a secondary composition) and in Ps. Sol. 5:1-2a; 17:1-4; 9:1-7. Also Add. Dan. 1:3-5 (praise of the righteous God).

In a few Psalms the introductory petition is missing and the remembrance of God's saving acts is so strong that the Psalm is introduced like declarative praise:

Ps. 89:1, "I will sing of thy steadfast love, O LORD, for ever."

The same is true of Isa. 63:7. This fact provides a simple explanation for the gradual mixture of style.[5]

This motif of the LP, then, could simply be a development of the divine predicates, which were reminders of God's actions, as for instance in Ps. 80:1; Gen. 48:15!

2. *The confession of trust.* Its place is between the lament and the petition: Pss. 74:12; 115:9-11; 85:6; 60:4-5a; 106:43-46; Isa. 64:8; Jer. 14:9b; Lam. 5:19. It is also encountered, however, following the petition or bound up with the petition, and this is always the case in the late Psalms (in some of which the lament has been omitted entirely), e.g., Isa. 63:16; 64:4b; Jer. 14:22; Add. Dan. 1:17c. The structure of Isa. 63:7—64:3 is questionable. A confession of sin precedes both of the other passages. In Ps. Sol. 7:4-5, where the confession of trust follows the petition, lament is completely lacking. There is a strange usage of the confession of trust in appositional phrases in the address at the beginning of some Psalms, Ps. 80:1; Jer. 14:8a; Ps. 85:4, or together with the vow of praise, Ps. 79:13a. Once it is even combined with the reference to God's former saving deeds, Ps. 44:4-8, and once it stands in its stead, Ps. 115:3.[6]

5. For this motif, cf. Wendel, *op. cit.,* p. 89. He finds the same motif in the prayer wishes (*Texts,* pp. 10 f.) in the divine predicates. "A divine predicate, such as 'God of Abraham' is intended to . . . obligate the deity. Such an expression was to work as a conjuration: 'Arise, Yahweh, who then didst show thyself so mighty.' "

6. It is completely lacking only in Ps. 83, in which lament and petition have only one subject, the foes.

The subject in these sentences can be God (usually addressed in the second person), or the people.

In these sentences Israel expresses its relation to God, from whom it expects acts of assistance. Most of the passages say that. But also the sentences in which Israel looks to God as shepherd, king, and father express this directly. For here the analogy of the relationships of this world tells what God is for his people.

The sentences that contain the vocabulary of trust say the same indirectly. It is to be noted that these are less common. A certain amount of reflection lies behind this vocabulary. The sentences which praise God's majesty or his compassion are also rare; they are similar to descriptive praise, while the main groups stand closer to declarative praise.

It was only in the latest period that the confession of trust passed into praise of the righteous God, as in Lam. 1:18, and throughout the Psalms of Solomon. This is connected with the fact that in the late Psalms of lament the lamentation is no longer so free and natural as in the earlier ones, but is more and more restricted by the recognition of one's own guilt on the one hand, and by the praise of the righteous God on the other.[7]

A clear boundary between confession of confidence and the praise of God cannot be drawn here. Most of these sentences, taken in themselves, are praise of the God who acts on behalf of his people. *In the confession of trust the lament of the peo-*

Examples of God addressed in the second person: Ps. 80:1; Jer. 14:8a; Pss. 85:6; 60:4-5a; Isa. 63:16; 64:4b; Jer. 14:9b; 14:22; Lam. 5:19; Ps. Sol. 5:5b; 7:4-5.
Of God addressed in the third person: Pss. 74:12; 115:3 (115:9-11); Lam. 1:18a. Of the people: Pss. 79:13a; 115:9-11; Add. Dan. 1:17c.
God is the one who acts (for his people): Pss. 74:12; 115:3; Isa. 64:4b; Jer. 14:22.
God is savior, redeemer, helper: Ps. 44:7; Jer. 14:8; Pss. 115:9-11; 85:4, 6; 60:4-5a; Isa. 63:16.
God is in our midst: Jer. 14:9b; is our God: Ps. Sol. 5:5.
God is the shepherd; his people, his flock: Pss. 80:1; 79:13a (74:1c).
God is Israel's king: Pss. 74:12; 44:4.
God is Israel's father: Isa. 63:16; 64:7 (cf. Heiler, *op. cit.*, p. 91, in primitive prayers).
God is hope; Israel trusts, hopes in him: Ps. 115:9-11; Isa. 64:3b; Jer. 14:22; Add. Dan. 1:17.
Israel rejoices in him: Ps. 85:6.
God is enthroned, reigns: Ps. 80:1; 115:3; Lam. 5:19.
God gives his people victory: Ps. 44:4.
God is merciful: Ps. Sol. 7:5.
God is righteous: Lam. 1:18; Ps. Sol. 8:23-26; 9:2b-5; 2:15-18 (praise!).
7. This process is an essential one for an understanding of the prehistory of the N.T. doctrine of justification.

ple is open toward praise. In Ps. 74 the confession of trust (12) introduces a P (13-17); and in Ps. 44, vss. 4-8 taken in themselves are an independent PP.

There is a difference here, however, from the "reference to God's former saving action." In the latter, reference is made to definite facts or data that lie in the past, while here the confidence in the previously experienced activity of God for his people is expressed in the present in faith and praise. The structure of those sentences was: "thou hast done . . . ," and the structure of these is: "thou doest . . ."

3. *Vow of praise and oracle of salvation.* In the LI the petition is followed by the vow of praise, which then often passes over into praise of God. Here therefore within a Psalm, lamentation is often turned into praise. In the canonical Psalms there are no LP that end in distinct praise of God, but some later ones do end this way.[8]

Moreover, the vow of praise is seldom met with in the LP. In the strict sense a vow was probably originally a matter for the individual, and thus the vow of praise has its proper place in the supplications and praise of the individual. In the Babylonian psalms too we never find a vow of praise in the plural.[9] It is therefore all the more to be noted that in the biblical Psalms such a vow is found several times. In Ps. 79:13 it stands in close connection with the confession of trust, and in Ps. 44:8 it forms the end of an expansion of the motif of vss. 1-3 into a PP in vss. 4-8.

In Pss. 106:47b; 80:18, and Ps. Sol. 8:33b it is connected with the petition in a final or a consecutive construction. In both passages an action is praised: "We shall not be moved. . . ." Likewise in the implied vows in Hos. 6:2 and Ps. 74:21b there is a jussive, and the clause sounds like an LI. Ps. 115 can be mentioned here only with reservations. It is a mixture of categories and the vow of praise in vss. 16-18 is characteristic of the LI. In some Psalms another look into the future stands in the

---

8. Ps. Sol. 8:34; Ecclus. 36.
9. Stummer, *op. cit.*, p. 117.

place of the vow of praise. The foes shall be brought to recognize (through God's intervention against them) that God is the Lord, e.g., Ps. 83:16b, 18; Ecclus. 36:5; 36:22b; Add. Dan. 22. Behind this Psalm ending there probably stands the expression so often used by Ezekiel, e.g., Ezek. 6:14; 7:27.[10]

It should be noted that the LP and the LI have in common the fact that in some way we are always pointed beyond mere lament and petition. They differ, however, in that this pointing beyond the present crisis does not have in the LP so definite a form as that of the vow of praise in the LI. This vow is occasionally met with, but not so frequently and not in so standardized a form. We cannot speak of it as a definite conclusion for a Psalm in the same way that we can in connection with the LI. In several Psalms the formulation of the vow of praise (e.g., Pss. 115:6-8; 74:21b) displays a similarity to the LI. In Pss. 79:13; 44:8; 106:47b, the wording is the same as that in the LI. Only Ps. 80:18 (cf. Ps. Sol. 8:33b) is different. According to Wendel, in the free prayers of the laity the only vow is that of an individual. All these factors then indicate that the vow of praise is by nature a part of the LI and was then borrowed as a motif for use in the LP.

The vow in Ps. 80, however, shows a striking relationship to the promise of the people at the assembly in Shechem, Josh. 24:16-18: vs. 18, "Therefore we also will serve the LORD, for he is our God" (and vs. 21); vs. 24, "The LORD our God we will serve, and his voice we will obey." It occurs here in another context, as answer to a question calling for a decision. We might inquire, however, whether this promise of the people at Shechem was an absolutely unique occurrence, or whether there is behind it a vow of the people that had its own fixed place in the cult.[11] Reference should be made here to Hos. 14:3, which contains a formal renunciation of other gods.

These Psalms end with a petition: Pss. 74; 84(?); 80(?); 89; Isa. 64:4-11; Jer. 14:1-10; Lam. 5, or with the confession of trust:

---

10. Or a similar clause found in Isa. 45:14; 45:6.
11. Pedersen makes a similar reference in *Israel*, III-IV, p. 661.

Jer. 14:13—15:4; Pss. 44(?); 80(?); 60; Isa. 63—64:3; Isa. 51:9-16.[12]

Where the vow of praise is lacking, the LP end either with a petition or with the confession of trust. Now, however, there is in some LP an entirely new and different part, which depicts God's answer to the supplications of his people. The answer can be affirmative or negative. That an unfavorable answer of God to the supplication of the people actually was conceivable is shown by Jer. 14:10 and 15:1-4, and also by Hos. 6:1-6. The transitional verse, Hos. 5:15, shows that this is intended to be an LP. It begins with the decision to repent, which is followed by a very detailed confession of trust. (This hints at a vow of praise.) Verses 4-6 give God's answer. Instead of the proclamation of salvation which the people awaited, "I will do unto you . . . ," there is the question, "What shall I do with you . . . ?" And this is based on the inconstancy of Israel. There follows in vs. 5 the (prophetic) proclamation of judgment with the reason for it in vs. 6.[13]

In all other passages God's answer is affirmative. The fact that an answer from God followed the LP can be seen more clearly in the prophetic books than in the LP contained in the Psalter. In addition to Jer. 14:15, there is in Jeremiah one other passage where an LP is clearly cited, Jer. 3:21 ff. In vs. 21 the lament of the people is given; in vss. 22b-25 we have the turning of the people to Yahweh with a confession of sins and an expression of trust. 4:1-2 is God's answer, a conditional proclamation of salvation. Between the portrayal of the lament and the turning to God there has been inserted a (prophetic) call to repentance.

Hos. 14 is very similar to this passage in Jeremiah. It seems

---

12. The question mark with Ps. 44 and Ps. 80 means that it is not possible to make a clear decision here. The final *sentence* in 44 is a petition, but the last words are, "for the sake of thy steadfast love." In Ps. 80 the final sentence is usually translated, "that we may be helped," or "that we may be saved." Luther translated, "so genesen wir" and the Zürich Bible, "so wird uns geholfen." According to Delitzsch in his commentary on this passage, both translations are possible. As for content, the passages which approach in form the vow of praise also belong in this group of Psalm endings, Ps. 83:18; Ecclus. 36:5, 22b; Add. Dan. 1:22. Behind the final or consecutive clause, "that they may know . . ." stands the belief that God is surely Lord.

13. Cf. H. Schmidt, "Hosea 6:1-6," *Sellin-Festschrift*, 1927, pp. 111 ff.

that a liturgy of penitence is the basis of both passages. In Hos. 14 the exhortation to petition for forgiveness of sin and for help, and also the indication of a vow of praise (vs. 3) have been inserted into the call to repent (vs. 2). Verse 4 quotes the renunciation of the foreign gods. Now follows in vss. 6-9 God's answer, which is here an unconditioned and very full proclamation of salvation, almost approaching the apocalyptic pictures of salvation.

In Ps. 85, as in the two just-mentioned passages, the petition is followed by a proclamation of salvation, introduced in vs. 8 as follows:

> Let me hear what God the LORD will speak,
> for he will speak peace to his people . . .

The sentences which follow depict rather than proclaim. In part they have many similarities with Hos. 14:6-9, and both actually speak more of the God who blesses than of him who intervenes to help.

The proclamation is very different in Ps. 60:6-9. Here God announces his victory over the nations who are Israel's foes (not at the End!). Isa. 33:10-13 is quite similar, " 'Now I will arise,' says the LORD . . ." (cf. Ps. 12:5). Gunkel refers to this connection between lament of the people and oracle of salvation on pp. 137 f., where he has collected a large number of examples. This approach was taken up by Begrich, "Das priesterliche Heilsorakel," ZAW 52, 1934, pp. 81-92. There, however, he dealt with it mainly as the answer to the lament of the individual. The answer of God to the lament of the people should be made the subject of a separate study.[14]

For our present investigation it is significant that the oracle of salvation often proclaims the coming intervention of God. (Begrich, op. cit., p. 8, "The message of Yahweh [is] addressed to the one seeking help, and speaks of his intervention.")

Isa. 33:10-13:

> " 'Now I will arise,' says the LORD . . ." (cf. Ps. 12:5).

Ps. 60:6-9:

14. Cf. Begrich, "Deuterojesaja-Studien," BWANT 4. F. H. 25, 1938: "Das Heils- oder Erhörungsorakel," pp. 6-19.

"With exultation I will divide up Shechem."
Isa. 49:22:
"Behold, I will lift up my hand to the nations, and raise my signal to the peoples."[15]
Isa. 59:15b f.: "The LORD saw it . . . He saw that there was no man . . . then his own arm brought him victory . . . He put on righteousness as a breastplate, and a helmet of salvation upon his head . . . he will come like a rushing stream . . . And he will come to Zion as Redeemer."
Jer. 51:36: "Therefore thus says the LORD: 'Behold I will plead your cause and take vengeance for you.' "
Mic. 7:11-13: "A day for the building of your walls!"
Hab. 3:3-15: "God came from Teman . . . He stood and measured the earth . . . Thou didst bestride the earth in fury . . . Thou wentest forth for the salvation of thy people."
Joel 2:1 ff.: "Blow the trumpet in Zion . . . Let all the inhabitants of the land tremble, for the day of the LORD is coming, it is near."

No fixed form is discernible. They have in common only the following features:

(a) They are oracles of salvation or occupy the place of such oracles.

(b) They all speak in some manner of God's intervention for the salvation of his people.

Two groups can be distinguished as follows:

1. Oracles of salvation as a word of Yahweh. He himself proclaims his intervention, as, for example, in Isa. 33:10-13. It is in this form that Second Isaiah took up the oracle of salvation.

2. This intervention of God is depicted in the third person. Isa. 59:13 ff.; Hab. 3:3-15; Joel 2:1 ff. belong to this group. These represent already a further development of the oracles of salvation. One of them is an epiphany, and the others are reminiscent of that form.

15. Begrich designates 24 passages as oracles of salvation or of God's hearing (*op. cit.*, p. 6). Every one of these contains the above-mentioned part in which God proclaims that he will intervene.

The variety of form of these oracles indicates a particular difficulty which should lead us to exercise the greatest caution. It is no accident that oracles of salvation are hardly ever found in the Psalter, but occur frequently, almost regularly, as answers to the laments of the people in the prophetic books. It is also no accident that the oracle of salvation is the most important literary form in Second Isaiah.

The answer to the lament of the people is communicated as God's answer by the priest or by the prophet. If it is combined with the lament of the people, we no longer have a Psalm in the strict sense, but a liturgy. In the designation "prophetic liturgy" the two component parts are clearly expressed.[16]

THE PSALM OF PETITION OR LAMENT OF THE INDIVIDUAL (LI)

The Parts:
> I. Address, with an introductory cry for help and/or of turning to God.
> II. Lament. (It has three subjects: Thou, O God . . . ; I . . . ; the foes . . .)
> III. Confession of trust. (Contrasted to the lament by the *waw* adversative.)
> IV. Petition: (a) for God to be favorable (look . . . incline thyself . . . hear . . .); (b) for God to intervene (help . . . save . . .).
> Motifs designed to move God to intervene.
> V. Assurance of being heard.
> VI. Double wish (wish or petition that God will intervene against . . . and for . . .).
> VII. Vow of praise.
> VIII. Praise of God (only where the petition has been answered!).

The following are the constituent parts of the LI: address, lament, confession of trust, or assurance of being heard, petition, vow of praise. This is the basic scheme, but it never becomes stereotyped. The possibilities of variation are unusually numerous.

16. Cf. Gunkel, *op. cit.*, pp. 136 ff., 329, 410 f.

When we consider the relationship of the praise of God to the petition of the individual, two questions arise: 1. What is the significance of the vow of praise in and for the Psalm of petition? 2. What is the significance of the oracle of salvation in and for the Psalm of petition?

Let us look at the second question first. Begrich's work "Das priesterliche Heilsorakel"[17] cast new light on the lament of the individual. The conclusions of this work are so clear and convincing that most of them have won general acceptance. Accordingly, as far as the lament of the individual is concerned we must reckon in every case with the possibility that the content is not only the lament and petition of the one who comes before God, that is, that he not only "pours out his heart" before Yahweh, but in some instances it is to be assumed that an oracle of salvation was given in the *midst* of the Psalm and that the Psalm also includes the words that follow the giving of the oracle. This conclusion had already been drawn for some Psalms, in which this can be seen with especial clarity. This explains the "abrupt change in mood" (Gunkel, *op. cit.,* p. 243) from lament to jubilation within a Psalm. But the consequences for the category as a whole have not yet been drawn. A group of Psalms within the category may then be distinguished. These are Psalms in which the oracle of salvation is to be assumed *in the middle,* and which contain not only what the petitioner says *before* the oracle, but also what he says after the oracle has been given. Thus these Psalms do not merely have something cheerful or trustful added, but the whole Psalm takes on a different character. Within these Psalms something decisive has occurred, something which changes what is being said here. This change will be pointed out in the Psalms involved.

Gunkel rightly said that the oracle of salvation as such is not a sufficient explanation of these Psalms (*op. cit.,* p. 247). In addition a real change must have taken place in the one speaking. It is therefore not the fact of the oracle as such that created this special type of Psalms of petition, but the word which in

17. *ZAW* 52, 1934, p. 43, note. Cf. Gunkel, *Einleitung,* pp. 245 ff. Fr. Küchler, "Das priesterliche Orakel in Israel und Juda," *Baudissin-Festschrift,* Giessen, 1918, p. 285.

Structure of the Psalm of Petition or Lament of the Individual

	142	102	27B
Address (Turning to God) Introductory cry for help	O LORD (first in vs. 5) I cry with my voice to the LORD	O LORD Hear my prayer Let my cry come to thee	O LORD Thy face, LORD, do I seek Hear!
Lament — Foes	They have hidden a trap for me	All the day my enemies taunt me	For false witnesses have risen against me
Lament — I	I look to the right There is none who takes notice of me	3-7, 9, 11 My days are like an evening shadow	————
Lament — Thou	————	Because of thy indignation For thou hast taken me up and thrown me away	(in anger)
Confession of trust	3a, 5 Thou art my refuge	12 ff. But thou, O LORD, art enthroned for ever	Thou who hast been my help O God of my salvation For my father and my mother . . . but the LORD

Petition	Heart	Give heed to my cry	(1-2)	Hide not thy face
	Save!	Deliver me from my persecutors	Take me not hence in the midst of my days	Give me not up to the will of my adversaries
Motifs		For I am brought very low For they are too strong for me	25-28 Thou dost endure	Because of my enemies
Vow of praise		That I may give thanks to thy name	—	—
Assurance of being heard		The righteous will surround me; for thou wilt deal	28? The children of thy servants shall dwell secure	I believe that I shall see the goodness of the LORD in the land of the living!

Structure of the Psalm of Petition or Lament of the Individual
(Petition has been heard)

		13	6	22
Address (Turning to God) Introductory cry for help		LORD	O LORD, rebuke me not Be gracious to me	My God, why?
Lament	Foes	How long shall my enemy be exalted over me?	—	(12-18) Surround me
	I	How long must I bear pain?	For I am languishing My bones are troubled (and 6-7)	(6-8) But I am a worm, and no man
	Thou	Wilt thou forget me for ever?	But thou, O LORD—how long?	(1-2) Why hast thou Thou dost lay me in the dust of death
Confession of trust		But I have trusted in thy steadfast love	For the sake of thy steadfast love	(3) Yet thou art holy (4-5) In thee our fathers trusted (9-10) Upon thee was I cast from my birth

		Consider and answer me	Turn	(11, 19) Be not far off
Petition	Hear!			
	Save!	Lighten my eyes	Save my life	19b-21 Hasten to my aid / Deliver my soul / Save me
	Punish!	——	——	——
Motifs		Lest my enemy say	For in death there is no remembrance of thee	There is none to help
Double wish		(4-5?)	(9-10)	——
Vow of praise		I will sing to the LORD	——	I will tell of thy name to my brethren (23 ff.)
(Declarative) Praise of God		Because he has dealt bountifully with me	Depart from me / For the LORD has heard	(24) For he has not despised / (31) He has wrought it

these oracles came from God to the one petitioning and lamenting. There is much evidence of this in the Psalms themselves, as for instance, Ps. 28:6, "He has heard the voice of my supplications." This word changes the one speaking. The one who speaks now has been transformed by God's having heard his supplication. Often even the moment of this change has been captured by a "now," or "but now," e.g., Pss. 27:6; 12:5 (God speaks); 20:6, "Now I know that the LORD will help" (cf. Ps. 119:67). Or God himself intervenes, Ps. 12:5.[18]

Usually the change is not so obvious. But there is an unequivocal mark that in the past has not been given sufficient attention. At the place where the change occurs, almost all of these Psalms contain a *waw* adversative, "But thou O God . . . ," or "But I . . ."

"But" (Waw Adversative) in the Lament of the Individual

But thou . . .

But I . . .

I. *In the lamentation*

Ps. 6:3: "But thou, O LORD—how long?"

Ps. 38:13: "But I am like a deaf man"

Ps. 70:5: "But I am poor and needy"

In a protestation of innocence:

Ps. 26:11: "But as for me, I walk in my integrity"

II. *In the petition*

Ps. 22:19: "But thou, O LORD, be not far off!"

Ps. 59:5: Thou, LORD God of hosts . . . awake"

Ps. 69:13: "But as for me, my prayer is to thee"

Ps. 55:16: "But I call upon God"

III. *As confession of trust* (after the lamentation) *or as assurance of being heard* (after the petition)

Ps. 22:3: "Yet thou art holy"

Ps. 102:12: "But thou, O LORD, art enthroned for ever"

Ps. 13:5: "But I have trusted in thy steadfast love"

Ps. 31:14: "But I trust in thee"

18. Compare the situation of the oracle in 1 Sam. 1 where this change is clearly expressed.

26: "But thou dost endure"
✓ 27: "But thou art the same"
Ps. 86:15: "But thou, O LORD, art a God merciful and gracious"
Ps. 3:3: "But thou, O LORD, art a shield"
✓ Ps. 55:23: "But thou, O God, wilt cast them down"
Ps. 59:8: "But thou, O LORD, dost laugh at them" (cf. Ps. 2:4)
✓ Ps. 109:28: "Let them curse, but do thou bless"
Ps. 64:7: "But God will shoot his arrow at them"
Isa. 38:17b: "But thou hast held back my life from the pit of destruction"

Ps. 52:8: "But I am like a green olive tree . . . I trust in the steadfast love of God"
Ps. 73:23: "Nevertheless I am continually with thee"
Ps. 27:6: "And now my head shall be lifted up"
Ps. 27:13: "[But] I believe that"
Ps. 35:9: "Then my soul shall rejoice in the LORD"
Ps. 71:14: "But I will hope continually"
Ps. 109:28: "[But] may thy servant be glad"
("Behold" instead of "but")
Ps. 54:4: "Behold, God is my helper"

The Waw *Adversative in the Petition of the Individual*

GRAMMATICAL OBSERVATION

It is necessary to imagine a conjunction that has not yet been differentiated into a copulative and an adversative.[19]

The *we'attah* can usually be translated in either of two ways: "and now" or "but now." Even where the *waw* is clearly adversative and is to be translated as "but," there remains a connection, even though only one of contrast. The contrast is actually made, not by the *waw*, but by the structure of the sentence. The *waw* always stands with the subject at the beginning of the sentence, as in Ps. 13:5: "But I—in thy steadfast love I have trusted" (order of the words in the Hebrew). This same contrast can occasionally take place without the *waw*. Ps. 17:15: "As for me, I shall behold thy face in righteousness." The contrast is therefore more deeply embedded in the structure of the sentence than by a conjunction only.

The *waw* adversative combined with the subject at the beginning of the clause indicates that here something else begins.   ✓

---

19. The German word "aber" once had this complex meaning. This is still shown by the words "abermals," and "tausend und abertausend." This was pointed out by Prof. Köhler.

This is especially clear when these clauses with "but" follow the lament. They indicate a transition from lamentation to another mode of speech, the confession of trust or the assurance of being heard.[20]

The attached table not only shows how numerous these clauses are, but also their vitality. No two of these sentences use the same words, and they never have a pre-determined form. The vitality of this form seems to me especially clear in the fact that expressions with the same meaning can occur in sentences whose subject is God as well as in sentences whose subject is "I." The transition which is expressed in all these sentences is one that occurs in a happening between God and man, and both are affected by it. It should be added that this transition is not schematically bound to any place in the Psalms. Its most frequent place is in connection with the "assurance of being heard," after the petition and before the vow of praise. But it can also stand earlier with the "confession of trust" between lament and petition. Often, to be sure, these two patterns coincide (as in Ps. 13:5). In addition, this clause with "but" is found a few times within the petition, and even in the midst of the lament. (See the table.) Here it cannot be said that it already indicates a transition, but it does likely already represent a contrast. In it we are already looking beyond the lament or the petition. The expression "but thou" is especially impressive in connection with the cry "How long?" in Ps. 6:3.

The clauses with "but thou . . ." The following observations should be taken in conjunction with Begrich's recognition of the significance of the oracle of salvation for the petition of the individual. The expression "but thou" usually marks the place at which in Ps. 12:5 the word from God stands, the place therefore at which the oracle of salvation occurs. We might even say it designates the oracle of salvation. If, however, it were necessary to think of each of these Psalms as standing in direct ritual connection with the oracle, this rite would have to have been defined by a much more fixed form. Yet even the "but clauses"

20. This is already found in prose prayers, as, e.g., Gen. 32:12.

in petitions and laments can scarcely be tied in with such a rite. In Ps. 22, for instance, the "but" is already clearly present in vs. 3 (after the first cry of dire need) and recurs in vs. 19 after the detailed lamentation. The actual turning point, however, comes between vs. 21 and vs. 22. In some Psalms (13; 22; 6; 28) it can readily be assumed that the oracle of salvation is actually to be pictured in the middle of the Psalm, but for others this is scarcely conceivable. The strongest argument is that it is not possible to make a clear and certain distinction between petitions that are "open" and those that have been heard. The rite of the oracle of salvation gives expression to the fact that God answers the one who cries to him. We must assume that what actually happened in the rite was not unconditionally bound to it and that it can be observed in the Psalms without being immediately accompanied by the rite (so also Gunkel).

It seems to me that a certain correspondence to these clauses with *but* can be found in two Egyptian petitions of the individual.[21] They are completely absent, as far as I can tell, in the Babylonian psalms. There we find in a few passages the "confession of trust," and some Egyptian psalms contain an "assurance of being heard," but the transition within the prayer which is indicated by the clauses with *but* occurs uniquely in the Psalms of Israel. In them there is the strongest witness to the reality of the help that is experienced, the condescending of God to the one who cries out to him.

The same sentence, which in Ps. 6:8 is the basis of the cry to the foes, "Depart!", is found again in Ps. 28:6, except that instead of that imperative we have here the shout of praise, "Blessed!" This "Blessed" therefore occupies here and in Ps. 31:21 the place of the "but." *These passages substantiate the fact that the "but" designates the transition from petition to praise within the Psalm of petition.* If this form of the *waw* adversative within the petition of the individual is peculiar to the Psalms of Israel, that means that here in the face of the still existing predicament the praise of God can be boldly sung in

21. See above p. 44. They are similar to the heard petitions of the Psalter.

the certainty that Yahweh in his heights (Ps. 22:3) has heard the one praying in the depths (28:6).[22]

The clauses with "but I . . ." The most frequent expression is, "But I have trusted thee" or similar words, e.g., Ps. 13:5; 31:14; 52:8; 27:13; 141:8; 38:15; 73:23.[23]

These clauses with "but I" are all confessions of trust. In each case they have in the whole of the Psalm exactly the same significance as the clauses with "but thou." There is no essential difference between the two groups. The sentence in Ps. 3:3, "But thou, O LORD, art a shield about me," does not say in its context anything different from Ps. 31:14, "But I trust in thee, O LORD." In Ps. 38:15 the two expressions stand together. Praise of God and confession of trust are very intimately related to each other in the clauses with "but."

The fact that confession of trust, certainty of being heard, and praise of God cannot be clearly distinguished here but merge with one another corresponds to the fact which has been mentioned earlier: no hard and fast boundary can be drawn in the category of petitions of the individual between petitions that have been heard and those that remain "open." It is an essential element in these Psalms that this boundary remain open. Now a further observation must be added.

In the investigation of all the LI of the Old Testament I found to my astonishment that there are no Psalms which do not progress beyond petition and lament! Ps. 143, which contains only lament and petition in its structure, still expresses clearly a confession of trust in the second half of each verse from vss. 8-10. There is a whole group of Psalms which contain neither the assurance of being heard, nor the vow of praise, nor a word of praise at the end, but not one of these Psalms, which consist essentially of only lament and petition, is entirely

22. In the N.T., John 11:41 is to be understood in precisely this way.
23. In Ps. 71:14 the "waiting" has taken the form of a vow of praise; similarly the words of rejoicing in Ps. 35:9; in Ps. 109:28 the "but" of the double wish is bound with the vocabulary of praise. A variation of the vow of praise is seen in "I shall behold thy face," Ps. 17:15. Instead of by "but," the caesura is marked by a new start which is contrasted with the previous one: "I know . . . ," Ps. 140:12; 56:9, or "I say . . . ," Ps. 140:6; 142:6; and once, "My heart is steadfast . . . ," Ps. 57:7.

without a glance beyond the present situation, even if only a half verse, which expresses a confession of trust. Between this type and, for instance, Ps. 22, which ends with a full, broad Psalm of praise, there are all the transitional steps imaginable.

In my opinion, this fact that in the Psalms of the O.T. there is no, or almost no, such thing as "mere" lament and petition, shows conclusively the polarity between praise and petition in the Psalms. The cry to God is here never one-dimensional, without tension. It is always somewhere in the middle between petition and praise. By nature it cannot be *mere* petition or lament, but is always underway from supplication to praise.

The Vow of Praise

The vow of praise is a constant component of the Psalms of petition (cf. the tables).[24] The position of the vow is at the end of the petition. That is, the petition passes over into the vow of praise. In the Psalms of petition of the individual the order of motifs seldom corresponds exactly to the schema. We have here such a large number of variations as almost to defy analysis, even when new motifs are scarcely added. It is thus all the more striking that almost without exception the vow of praise maintains its fixed place at the end of the petition. This shows the power and consistency of this motif.

The same holds true for the structure of the motif itself. It is almost always a voluntative with the subject "I" and the object "God," thus a single, invariable clause. The possibilities for variation are to be sought in the vocabulary. The typical

24. Where it is lacking, it is either present in a different form, "I shall behold thy face in righteousness; when I awake, I shall be satisfied with beholding thy form," Ps. 17:15 (as also in the Babylonian psalms); "I will rejoice," Ps. 31:7, or it has been transformed into a report, Ps. 73:28, or an exhortation, Pss. 27:14; 31:24, or into a future condition, 43:4. Traces of it are there in Pss. 6:5; 88:10-12, where it is said as a motif to gain the desired result that in Sheol God can no longer be praised. Cf. Isa. 38:18 f. Its place can also be taken by another consequence of God's intervention, Ps. 58:11. Or, in some cases its absence is motivated by the structure of the Psalm, especially there where praise itself has already taken the place of the vow of praise, "Blessed be the LORD," Pss. 28:6; 31:23 f. We find declarative praise in Pss. 6:8-9; 10:17; and descriptive praise in Pss. 10:16-18; 12:6; 102:24b-27. It is completely absent in Pss. 143; 141; 38; 25 (alphabetic Psalm); 58, and the above-mentioned Psalms in which another form is substituted for it. It is omitted from the Psalms of trust, but even in them there are still clear traces of the vow of praise, Pss. 73:28; 23:6b.

verb for this vow of praise is *hōdāh*. Only in exceptions which are mostly late does there appear in its stead or alongside of it one of the other expressions for praise. On the other hand there is often an accompanying word, especially, "I will sing."

More precise designations provide other possibilities for variations. A survey of all the voluntative expressions (inclusive of those at the beginning of Psalms) gives the following results:

1. The original form of the vow of praise contained only *one* verb. Where more are to be found, it is to be assumed that the Psalm is later. Those Psalms in which the voluntative form is particularly numerous are certainly late, as, e.g., Ps. 71.

2. The only specific designation that is certainly original is that of the place, "before the congregation," etc. This is often found in the Babylonian psalms. The specific designations of the extent of time, such as "for ever," are certainly late.

3. It can be assumed with assurance that the oldest form of the vow of praise is the simple voluntative with God as the object, and followed by a statement of the reason for the vow. An example is Ps. 13:6: "I will sing to the LORD, because he has dealt bountifully with me."

What is the significance of the vow of praise? We should first of all recall that this vow is common to both the Psalms of the Old Testament and those of Babylon. Moreover, it is also to be found in those of Egypt (see above, pp. 38-39, 46).

It is certain that the vow of praise originally was connected with a vow to offer sacrifice. In the Psalms, the vows of praise show this by a polemical addition such as that in Ps. 51:16 ff. and Ps. 69:31. In addition, both could be included in one vow, as Ps. 27:6 and Ps. 54:6. Ps. 66:13-16 shows sacrifice and praise side by side in the fulfillment of a vow. In the Babylonian sources that have been preserved the vows of praise far outnumber those of sacrifice.

Moreover, the vow of praise is encountered even in primitive prayers. A Khoikhoi prayer (Heiler, *Das Gebet,* p. 159) reads, "Thou, O Tsuiga . . . thou art our father . . . Let our herds live, let us live . . . O that we might praise thee. . . ."

The attempt to interpret the vow of praise as a spiritualizing of an original vow of sacrifice does not correspond to the facts. The vow of praise has not simply taken the place of one of sacrifice. In any case, that is not the whole story. Praise is not a substitute for sacrifice, but had its own original meaning along-side of sacrifice. Sacrifice is food for the god; praise, however, belongs to the life of the god as much as does food. This is to be thought of in much the same way as the fact that man cannot exist without food, but also not without some recognition, some "honor." Thus both parallel each other back into very early times.

But just what meaning does the vow have? Why does a vow belong at the end of a petition? For us "vow" contains an ele-ment of the solemn, of the extraordinary, which conceals from us the real meaning of the word. There is really no difference at all between "to promise" and "to vow." The form could equally well be called a "promise of praise." It is a witness to an understanding of existence in which man does not yet stand alone, or need God only for his religious requirements. The vow of praise is the link between petition and praise. It closes the circle from petition to praise. It is one of the sure signs that the petition does not arise out of itself or out of some lack in the one petitioning, but out of the polarity of petition and praise.

The vow of praise does not correspond to thanks but to the praise of God. This is expressed especially in the specific state-ments such as the following:

> Ps. 22:22: "I will tell of thy name to my brethren; in the midst of the congregation I will praise thee."
> Ps. 22:25: "in the great congregation; . . . before those who fear him."
> Ps. 26:12b: "in the great congregation."
> Ps. 27:5b: "under the cover of his tent."
> Ps. 57:9: "among the peoples; . . . among the nations."
> Ps. 71:18: "till I proclaim thy might to all the generations to come."

To praise is to speak, to tell, to proclaim, to magnify his glory. It is telling abroad God's great deeds, just as it is said at the beginning of the proclamation of the apostles of Jesus Christ, Acts 2:11. *The concept and the reality of proclamation have one of their roots in the forensic element of the praise of God, as it is expressed particularly in the vow of praise.*

Because the petition for continuity more and more took the place of the cry out of dire need, the vow of praise lost its importance and finally disappeared entirely. It was no longer regarded as necessary. This can be seen in the Babylonian prayer literature and even more clearly in that of Egypt, where the petition for continuity is absolutely dominant and, correspondingly, the vow of praise is seldom encountered. It is probably generally true that in the late period of a religion, prayers expressing continuity outnumber those which arise from the cry of dire momentary need, and finally largely or entirely displace them. This process can also be observed in the petitionary Psalms of the O.T. But just at the point where this almost necessary development is recognized we are astonished to see to what extent, even down to the latest period, the petition in the midst of tribulation, the cry from the depths, is dominant in the Psalms. For this reason the vow of praise is appropriate and remained alive throughout the period in which Psalms were written. The fitting place for the vow of praise was alongside the cry of need. A feeling that this is so has remained everywhere down to the present. Whoever truly cries to God out of the depths, and in this cry thinks not of his need but of God (cf. the dual nature of the petition, "Hear!" and "Save!") knows that the moment of making a vow, a promise, is a part of this cry. I *know* then that the matter is not finished when I have pled and God has heard, but that something else must still come. I know that I owe something to God. It is totally false to belittle this as a bargain, as a *do ut des.* On the contrary, it is only through the promise that I bind to my petition that the petition gains its weight and value. I know that with the promise that I add to my petition I have entered into a relationship with God.[25]

25. The Roman Catholic practice of vows contains a reminder of the original reality of vows. Luther's vow at Stotternheim, "Help, holy St. Anna, and I will

The Transition to Declarative Praise

The fact that lamentation and petition can change into praise in the same Psalm has as a consequence a development which is peculiar to the Israelite Psalms, i.e., that praise is already heard in the conclusion of lament and petition, and that it forms the basis for the vow of praise.[26]

> Ps. 13:6: "I will sing to the LORD, because he has dealt bountifully with me" (cf. 22:31).
> Ps. 3:7: "For thou dost smite."
> Ps. 10:17: "Thou wilt hear" (or, hast heard).
> Ps. 6:8: "Depart . . . for the LORD has heard."
> Ps. 54:7: "For thou hast delivered me from every trouble."
> Ps. 56:13: "For thou hast delivered my soul from death."
> Ps. 31:7: "I will rejoice . . . because thou hast seen my affliction."
> Ps. 28:6: "Blessed be the LORD! for he has heard the voice of my supplications."
> Ps. 31:21: "For he has wondrously shown his steadfast love to me."
> Ps. 22:24: "For he has not despised or abhorred."

In order for the contrast which governs each of these Psalms to become clear it would be necessary to hear all these statements in the direct context of the loudest lament or most urgent entreaty of the same Psalm. It should be noted that the grief over which the suppliant is lamenting, and for the removal of which he pleads with God, still remains. During the praying of these Psalms no miracle has occurred, but something else has occurred. God has heard and inclined himself to the one praying; God has had mercy on him. (See the passages cited.)

---

become a monk," is a typical example of the way in which this outlook was so dominant then.

It is characteristic, however, that in the Roman Church the vow of praise has been almost entirely displaced by the vow of works. Franz Werfel's novel *The Song of Bernadette* is excellent evidence of the vitality of this vow even in the present day.

26. A corresponding reason following the vow of praise is never found in the LP.

And in this the decisive event has taken place. That which is yet to come, the turning point in the situation, must of necessity follow. Therefore it can now already be regarded as realized.

This transition is the real theme of the Psalms which are being discussed here. *They are no longer mere petition, but petition that has been heard. They are no longer mere lament, but lament that has been turned to praise.*

There is a difficulty, in that, as has been mentioned, this group of Psalms cannot be exactly delimited. In addition to those already listed (Pss. 3; 6; 10; 13; 22; 28; 31A; 31B; 54; 56) I should like to include here Isa. 38:10-20;[27] Pss. 27A; 64. Those which stand in the middle between open and heard petition are Pss. 12; 5; 86; 102; 69; 71; 7; 35A. The transition from the LI to the Psalms of confidence is seen in Pss. 73; 130; 123, and the transition to a didactic Psalm similar to Ps. 1, in Ps. 52.

This fluidity of transition, however, is one of the essential elements in these Psalms. They are all on the way from petition or supplication and lament to praise. It is not possible to determine the points at which they stand on this road. Even the Psalms that are open petition, petition before the turning point in the situation, and end with the vow of praise or a petition, as Pss. 141; 142; 55; 9:13-14; 61; etc., do not *only* stand on that side of the turning point but already anticipate it in the certainty of being heard or in a confession of confidence.

Thus it is that the picture of the Psalter which we find in contemporary research is changed at one point. Scholars have spoken of the absolute preponderance of Psalms of petition, and Gunkel explained this through the frailty of the human heart, which is quick enough to ask, but which readily forgets to thank. When the category which has up till now been called "Song of Thanks of the Individual" is compared with the songs of lament of the individual that judgment is correct. But this comparison is unjustifiable. A major portion of the LI consists of heard

27. The so-called "Psalm of Thanks of Hezekiah" has quite clearly the structure of these heard petitions, and not that of the declarative Psalm of praise or Psalm of thanks!

petitions. Within these Psalms lamentation has been turned into praise. They already contain the "thanks." All these Psalms, in which lament and petition end in a statement that is already declarative praise are rather witnesses to the power of the praise of God, which can well up from the depths. It is no longer possible to speak of an absolute predominance of petition and lament. Rather, precisely this group of heard petitions becomes a powerful witness to the experience of God's intervention, intervention that is able to awaken in the one lamenting, while his sorrow is materially unchanged, the jubilant praise of the God who has heard the suppliant and come down to him.

THE DECLARATIVE PSALM OF PRAISE OF THE PEOPLE (PP)

This category[28] is the most difficult of all. What is presented here can be only tentative. We found a firm connection between the lament and the praise of the individual in the final part of the LI (assurance of being heard), where lamentation was already turned into praise, "for God has heard," "for he has done . . ." There is no such connection between the lamentation and the praise of the people. The corresponding part is found only in very late Psalms (Ps. Sol. 7:6-10; 9:9-11). Perhaps this lack can be explained in that the supplication of the people in a time of national calamity, especially of defeat and its consequences, *could not* be turned so quickly into praise as the supplication of the individual out of his personal need.

Although the predominance of lament over praise in the Psalms of the individual found a simple explanation in the fact that a great many of the LI are petitions that have already been heard and therefore contain the praise of the one who is sure of deliverance, the same cannot be said of the Psalms of the people. This is all the more significant in that there are very few Psalms of praise of the people, as separate Psalms only 124 and 129, which belong to the little collection of the *Ma'alot* Psalms (Psalms of ascent), 120-134. How is this to be explained? It is all but impossible that there can have been as little declara-

28. Gunkel, *Einleitung*, "Danklied Israels," pp. 315 ff.

tive praise of the people, of jubilant, joyous relating of what God had done for his people, as appears from the Psalter as it has come down to us. Why, here we are dealing with the fundamental relationship of Israel to her God! What can be the basis of the fact that the category of the Psalms which has precisely this as its own theme is represented with such striking rarity in the Psalter?

One reason is probably that the Psalter as we now have it is a postexilic collection. The time in which Israel experienced God's wonderful intervention in *history* lies in the distant past. To be sure, the remembrance of those saving deeds of God remained constantly alive. The praise of God, however, which was uttered directly under the influence of God's saving deed which had just occurred, was preserved, insofar as it was handed on at all, only a few places in the Psalter.

There is, though, in the Psalter a strong, indirect witness to the immediate praise of God for his deeds on behalf of his people, though this praise was not transmitted: those parts of the LI which look back on the earlier saving activity of God. (See above, p. 55.) They contain echoes of that praise that was once awakened in direct response to what God had done.

Another reason could be the fact that this declarative praise of the people stood in the middle between the conventional expression of the Psalms (poetry) and a simple report. There are many indications of this, and they will be considered presently.

There is, however, in addition to this first difficulty of the extremely limited number of Psalms that have been preserved, a second. These few Psalms belong to different groups. They belong first of all to the two groups which Gunkel distinguished in his *Einleitung* as "Song of Thanks of Israel" (pp. 315 ff.) and "Song of Victory" (pp. 311 ff.). They have in common that almost every word is filled with the joy which has been released. God has helped us—we are saved! The following three features recur in each of the songs:

1. God has acted; let him be praised!

2. Praise is a direct response to the act which has just occurred.

3. Praise is expressed joyously.

Moreover the occasion for praising God is essentially the same in both groups: God has delivered his people in a marvelous manner from the threats of their foes.[29]

The only difference between the two groups is that in the Psalms of praise of the people there is no allusion to a battle that preceded the deliverance, while the report of battle and victory is a component part of the song of victory. Thus there is an appreciable difference between Ps. 124, a detailed song of praise of the people, and Judg. 5, a detailed song of victory. This difference disappears, however, in those songs of both groups which consist of only one or two sentences, that is, where God's saving act or the victory is only alluded to but not recounted. This can be seen on the one hand in Exod. 15:21 and on the other hand in Judg. 16:23 f. In these very brief songs that distinction is no longer of any significance.

To these two groups must be added the epiphanies, that is, Psalms or parts of Psalms in which God's coming to the aid of his people is depicted. It is a question, however, whether they represent originally independent Psalms or whether they were from the beginning a part of a Psalm, a motif. Such an epiphany is found as a part of a Psalm in the song of victory, Judg. 5 (vss. 4-5), and in Ps. 18 (vss. 7-18), which resembles a song of victory, and in addition in many other Psalms and in passages in the prophetic literature. Ps. 114[30] and Ps. 29 are the only epiphanies which are independent Psalms (but these are greatly modified).

Pss. 124; 129; Exod. 15:21; Ps. 66:8-12; Isa. 26:13-19; Ps. Sol. 13:1-4, fall in this category. Motifs or allusions are found in Deut. 32:43; Pss. 44:4-8; 66:6; 81:6-7; 85:1-3; 93:3-4; 126:2-3;

29. Gunkel, op. cit., p. 316, "The most frequent occasions of thank festivals in Israel are political in nature."
30. This is questionable. LXX reads 114 and 115 as a single Psalm. Ps. 77:13-20 is combined with an LI.

144:9-10; Isa. 25:1-5 (a mixed form of PI and PP); Isa. 25:9; 2 Macc. 15:34; Judg. 13:17; Luke 1:68-75.

Ps. 124 and Ps. 129 have essentially the same structure and display great similarity in other respects. The main part is the report of deliverance (here they agree even in the metaphor used!): Pss. 124:6, 7; 129:4.

In both Psalms this is preceded only by an allusion that glances back at the time of need. Both are introduced by a jussive after the initial clause, "Let Israel now say." Ps. 118 begins in the same manner. In Ps. 124:7a the report of deliverance is followed by a short sentence which tells the consequence of God's act for the one freed, and this is expanded by a picture; in Ps. 129:5-8 it is followed by the consequences of God's act for the foes.[31]

If the repetitions and expansions through figures of speech are omitted in Ps. 124, the following two sentences remain (1a+3a+6):

> "If it had not been the LORD who was on our side, then they would have swallowed us up alive." "Blessed be the LORD, who has not given us as prey to their teeth!"

In Ps. 129 it is even clearer that these two sentences are the core of the Psalm. Here vss. 1-2 are a summarizing introduction (as in the PI!), and the body of the Psalm (vss. 3-4) then consists of only the two sentences:

> "The plowers plowed upon my back; they made long their furrows. The LORD is righteous; he has cut the cords of the wicked."

In my opinion these two Psalms demonstrate the simplest and most original way of praising God. Yahweh has acted. He has broken the bonds with which his people were bound. For this reason praise is uttered. It consisted of a simple declarative sentence, to which may be added the shout of praise, *"bārūk yahweh!"*

---

31. Ps. 129:8b is probably an addition. Ps. 124:8, a confession of confidence, is only loosely connected to the Psalm, even if it originally was a part of it.

The Psalm of Praise of the People

	Exodus 18:10	Exodus 15:21	Ps. 126:3, 4	Ps. 144:9, 10
Shout of praise	Blessed be the LORD	Sing to the LORD	(2, 3) We are glad	I will sing a new song to thee, O God.
Report of God's act	Who has delivered you out of the hand of the Egyptians	He has triumphed gloriously; the horse and his rider he has thrown into the sea	The LORD has done great things for us	Who givest victory to kings, who rescuest David thy servant

	Ps. 124	Ps. 129	Ps. Sol. 13:1-4
Exhortation	Let Israel now say	Let Israel now say	———
Introductory summary	If it had not been the LORD who was on our side	Sorely have they afflicted me . . . yet they have not prevailed	(1, 2) The Lord's right hand has preserved us

Looking back on the time of need	When men rose up against us . . . then they would . . . then over us would have gone	The plowers plowed upon my back	(3) Wild beasts have fallen upon them
Praise	Blessed be the LORD	The LORD is righteous	
Report of God's acts	Who has not given us as prey to their teeth! We have escaped!	He has cut the cords of the wicked	But out of all that the Lord has freed us!
	(8) Confession of confidence	(5-8) Wishes against Zion's foes	

The sentences to which the 124th Psalm were reduced no longer give an unconditional impression of a fixed mode of speech. They sound more like a prose report. Here it can be seen that the PP is still very near to the simple report. Only the sentence Ps. 124:6 (the σκόπος of this Psalm) resembles in its structure and in its meaning a sentence which is often encountered in the historical books, e.g.: Exod. 18:10, "Blessed be the LORD, who has delivered you out of the hand of the Egyptians." But it may also occur without the *bārūk*:

2 Sam. 5:20, "And he [David] said, 'The LORD has broken through my enemies before me, like a bursting flood.' "[32]

These sentences show the same three elements which are in general determinative for declarative praise:

1. The praise of Yahweh for a deed that he has done.
2. The nature of these sentences as *immediate* response to God's intervention.
3. The essentially joyful nature of this praise.[33]

In their structure (shout of praise and the reason for it: God has acted) *as well as in these three elements the bārūk sentences in the historical books correspond to the declarative Psalms of praise.* In the declarative Psalms of praise these simple sentences which were born in the moment when help was experienced have become songs.[34]

This connection between the Psalms and the historical reports is further strengthened by the fact that of all the vocabulary of praise only this form of the verb *bārak* (with God as object) is encountered in both places. No other form of any of the vocabulary of praise is encountered in both the historical books and the Psalms.

Here we can recognize the point at which the praise of God in its simplest form is to be found in the midst of the history of

32. Similarly, Gen. 14:19 f.; 1 Sam. 25:32 f., 39; 2 Sam. 18:28; Gen. 24:27; 1 Kings 1:48; 5:21; 10:9; Ruth 2:19 f.; 4:14 f. For the formula, see R. Kittel, *PRE³* XVIII, p. 154.
33. Similarly, Wendel, *Laiengebet,* pp. 170 ff.
34. *Ibid.,* p. 188. Structure: I, Praise; II, Recounting of Praise. "The Hymns show, principally, the same structure."

God's people as reported in the historical books. We can recognize in these sentences the most original and immediate form of the praise of God, the simple and joyous response to a definite act of God which has just been experienced. For this form of the praise of God we can say in any case that its origin is *not* the cult. This praise of God accompanies God's great deeds as their necessary echo:

> Ps. 106:8, 11-12, "Yet he saved them for his name's sake, that he might make known his mighty power." "And the waters covered their adversaries; not one of them was left. Then they believed his words; they sang his praise."

There was no need here for any intermediate step, any arrangement, any particular representation. God's great deeds awaken praise, and this can be expressed in *one* sentence.[35]

There are then many ways in which this one sentence can be varied, repeated, adorned, or developed. Still, the essence of the matter remains contained in the one sentence, as can be seen in Ps. 124 and Ps. 129. The nearer this praise is to God's deed, the shorter and simpler it will be.

The road by which praise moved from this simplest stage to the great descriptive Psalms of praise (hymns) can be seen in miniature with singular clarity in the history of those *bārūk* sentences of which we have spoken above. In the original stage they agree with the sentences in the Psalms.[36] Two passages from Solomon's prayer at the dedication of the temple, 1 Kings 8:14 f. and 55 f., illustrate the second stage. Here the *bārūk* does not follow directly on God's actions, but is rather reserved for the feast day, the great day of the dedication of the temple. One of the three elements, the "today," is here in the background. As a consequence of this, the praise is directed not only to a specific act of God, but to an act that extends over a longer period of time. "Blessed be the LORD who has given rest to his people Israel, according to all that he promised" (1 Kings 8:56). The final

35. Köberle, "Die Motive des Glaubens an die Gebetserhörung im A.T.," Leipzig, 1901. He regards the deliverance from Egypt as the most important of these motifs, pp. 15, 20, 23.
36. Thus Pss. 124:6; 68:19; 28:6; 66:20; 18:46; 144:1.

stage can be seen in the doxologies that conclude the books of the Psalter.[37]

Here there is no concrete occasion for praise. The cry of praise, *bārūk*, has been entirely removed from the historical scene and is a timeless liturgy. In the place of the very simple language of the *bārūk* sentences there now appears in Ps. 72:18 f., for example, a developed, liturgically full, and solemn language, and these sentences become like the heavy, golden implements of an altar.

The fact that the *bārūk* sentences of the earlier stage resemble the central part of the declarative Psalms of praise points to the possibility that there were Psalms of praise of the people which were contained in one sentence. Such a Psalm has been preserved in what is apparently the oldest Psalm of Israel, the so-called Song of Miriam, Exod. 15:21:

> "Sing to the LORD, for he has triumphed gloriously;*
> the horse and his rider he has thrown into the sea."[38]

This sentence is a typical declarative Psalm of praise with the cry of praise and the reason for it, God's deed. Here we do not find the looking back to the time of need as a separate part of the Psalm, and it is only hinted at in the second sentence, which is an explication of God's act. Exod. 15:21 contains the three elements (see above) which constitute the essence of declarative praise. The twofold nature of the sentence is to be observed. The second part reports the saving deed itself, and the first part gives the action of God which led to it. This corresponds to the double request, for God to turn to the one praying ("Arise!") and for God's intervention. The former is expressed in a singular manner in Exod. 15:21; the verb is not used in connection with God elsewhere in the O.T. (although its derivatives are), and it is to be understood in a sense similar to that of *qūm*, which is often applied to God both in laments and in praise.

37. Pss. 41:13; 72:18 f.; 89:52; 106:48 (=41:13).
* Westermann translates here "denn hoch hat er sich erhoben," "for he has arisen on high."
38. LXX reads, "Let us sing," probably correctly.

A sentence from a Psalm of the time of the exile, Ps. 126:3, is similar to the Song of Miriam, "The LORD has done great things for us; we are glad." This sentence shows that the basic character and the simple structure of the declarative Psalm of praise were preserved down to that period.[39]

THE SONGS OF VICTORY

Judg. 5; 16:23 f.; Pss. 118:15 f.; (149?); Judith 16.
Motifs of the songs of victory are found in Pss. 68; 18; 149; Exod. 15; Deut. 32.

As far as the songs which consist of a single sentence are concerned it is hardly possible to stress any difference between this group and the former one. Exod. 15:21 is certainly no song of victory, because no battle took place, but it can scarcely be separated from those short songs of victory, which are to be recognized as such by the situation in which they arose.

Thus there has been transmitted to us in its original form what is probably a very old song of the Philistines which they sang when they had overcome Samson:

Judg. 16:23 f., "Our god has given Samson our enemy into our hand."

In verse 24 the song is given once again, now expanded by a twofold designation of "our enemy," which in content corresponds to the element of "looking back to the time of need":

". . . the ravager of our country,
who has slain many of us."

This small variation gives an indication of the way in which a song which originally consisted of a single sentence, or rather a mere shout of joy, could gradually grow into a song. It shows

---

39. There are two indications that this declarative praise of God was really much more frequent and varied than the sources would now lead us to believe. The first of these is the constant feature of the historical books, where after a marvelous, saving act of God a memorial is set up (e.g., 1 Sam. 14:35, and Josh. 4:20-23). This memorial was intended to bear witness to God's saving action. The other indication is the personal names, of which a great many have the significance of declarative praise, not only of the individual, but also of the people. Cf. Noth, *Die israelitischen Personennamen*, Stuttgart, 1928; Greiff, *Das Gebet im A.T.*, Münster, 1915, p. 93.

also that looking back to the time of dire need is not necessarily a part of it, but is rather the first expansion which the simple sentence underwent.

The Song of Deborah, the only extensive song of victory from pre-exilic times that has been transmitted fully, shows by its structure that it is similar to the Psalms of praise of the people, or that it is a type of Psalm of praise of the people.

Judg. 5: 2-3: Exhortation to praise Yahweh.
          4-5: Portrayal of the epiphany of God.
          6-8: Looking back at the time of need.
          9-11: New introduction (a call to praise God).
          12-30: Account of the victory.
          31: God's foes—God's friends.

The Song of Deborah, moreover, contains many of the traits that are associated with the "Holy War."[40]

Israel's songs of victory from the early period were likely connected closely with the wars of Yahweh. The early end of this institution must be the reason that so few of them have been preserved.[41] It is to be assumed that the "Book of the Wars of Yahweh" also contained Israelite songs of victory. On the basis of the material that has been transmitted, it seems reasonable to conclude that praise of Yahweh for the victory was an essential part of the wars of Yahweh. Just as the Song of Deborah is a part, namely the conclusion of one of the wars of Yahweh, so the Song of the Philistines, Judg. 16:23 f., has come down to us as a part of the celebration in a service of worship after the overcoming of the foe. The expression of this short song, "Our god has given into our hand . . . ," has been shown by von Rad to be a statement connected with the holy war (*op. cit.*, pp. 7 f.). The same seems to be the case with the statement of Saul that concludes the battle in 1 Sam. 11:13, ". . . for today the LORD has wrought deliverance in Israel." Praise of God for victory is also preserved in a very late passage, 2 Chron. 20:26.[42]

40. Cf. von Rad, *Der Heilige Krieg im alten Israel,* Zürich, 1951, pp. 18 ff.
41. *Ibid.*, p. 33.
42. Cf. *ibid.*, p. 80 f.

The sentence in 1 Sam. 11:13 is very close to Ps. 118:15 f. where we have echoes of a song of victory:

Hark, glad songs of victory in the tents of the righteous:
"The right hand of the LORD does valiantly,
the right hand of the LORD is exalted,
the right hand of the LORD does valiantly!"

Allusions to the song of victory are found frequently. Ps. 68, above all, is permeated by the motifs of these songs: vss. 1-4 (cf. Judg. 5:31!); 8-9 (epiphany of God); 11-14; 17-18; 20; 22-23; 35. In Ps. 18, an epiphany of God has been inserted into a PI (vss. 7-15), and vss. 32-48 are probably a sharply modified portion of a song of victory. In Deut. 32, vss. 40-43 are reminiscent of a song of victory, as are vss. 65-66 in Ps. 78. It can also be said of Ps. 149 that it contains echoes of a song of victory in vss. 4-9.[43]

The original form of the song of victory, looking back to the time of need, the report of the victory, and the praise of God, can no longer be recognized here. On the other hand, Judith 16:2-21 shows the revival of the song of victory in very late times with the old structure. There is, however, a very distinctive difference between it and Judg. 5; in Judith there is no battle! Judith alone did the deed (vss. 7-11) that put the foes to flight (vss. 12-13), and the only task the men had was to kill the fleeing enemies (vs. 14). Here too there is a feature of the epiphany (vs. 18). The conclusion, vss. 19-21, corresponds to Judg. 5:31.

Gunkel (op. cit., p. 341) draws attention to the fact that when there were again victories in Israel in very late times, "hymns" replaced songs of victory, and he refers to 1 Macc. 13:48-51 and 2 Macc. 3:30. The same could be said of 2 Chron. 20:26. In the later history of Israel the song of victory could live on only as an eschatological song that anticipated the coming victory of Yahweh. But no distinctive development took place here. It was also a set motif in some of the Zion Psalms, in which a victory of Yahweh over his foes before his city Zion was celebrated.

43. Gunkel regarded this Psalm as an eschatological hymn that had been written for the future victory feast (see his commentary on this passage).

This is seen above all in Ps. 48:2-8; in Pss. 46:4-7; 76:3-6, and perhaps also in Ps. 68.

These motifs of the eschatological songs of victory are very close to the enthronement Psalms. Both are Psalms of expectation. God's entry into his kingship, however, is not connected with a victory of God, but with a day of judgment of the nations.

THE EPIPHANY OF GOD

Judg. 5:4-5; Ps. 18:7-15; Hab. 3:3-15; Pss. 68:7 f., 33; 77:16-19; 97:2-5; 114; 29; 50:1-3; Deut. 33; Isa. 30:27-33; 59:15b-20; 63:1-6; Mic. 1:3-4; Nah. 1:3b-6; Zech. 9:14; Judith 16:18.

It is striking that in the few songs of victory that have been preserved there is often connected a portrayal or at least an allusion to the epiphany of God. Judg. 5:4-5; Pss. 68:7-8, 33; 18:7-15; Judith 16:18 (cf. Zech. 9:15 following vs. 14). That which unites them is God's intervention to help his people. When he intervenes in this way, God appears from afar (epiphany), and he fulfills his purpose by gaining victory for his people (song of victory). Thus in Judg. 5 there follows on the epiphany (vss. 4-5) the report of victory. It is therefore reasonable to assume that the epiphanies were originally parts of Psalms, and do not represent independent Psalms.[44]

Judg. 5:4-5 begins, "LORD, when thou didst go forth from Seir" (or, "When thou goest out"). Thus also Ps. 68:7. Similar are Hab. 3; Deut. 33; Isa. 30; Mic. 1:5; Nah. 1:3. The beginning of the epiphany resembles unmistakably the epiphany of a god in the Babylonian and Egyptian psalms. For example:

The great hymn to Shamash, VR 50 and 51, Stummer, *op. cit.*, p. 40, Zimmern A, p. 15:

"Shamash, when thou goest forth from thy great mountain,
The great gods come before thee to judgment. . . ."
Hymn K 256 (also IV R 17), Stummer, *op. cit.*, p. 41:

---

44. Further evidence is the fact that they can be occasionally heard in the laments of the people; see above, p. 63.

The Epiphany of God

	Hab. 3:3-15	Judg. 5:4-5	Ps. 18:7-15
God comes from . . .	God came from Teman and the Holy One from Mount Paran	Lord, when thou didst go forth from Seir, when thou didst march from the region of Edom	He bowed the heavens, and came down; thick darkness was under his feet
The earth quakes	He stood and measured the earth; he looked and shook the nations	The earth trembled	Then the earth reeled and rocked
Mountains quake	Then the eternal mountains were scattered, the everlasting hills sank low	The mountains quaked before the Lord	The foundations also of the mountains trembled
Upon horses and chariots	Was thy wrath against the rivers? When thou didst ride upon thy horses, upon thy chariot of victory	—	He rode on a cherub and flew . . . upon the wings of the wind

Streams of water	Thou didst cleave the earth with rivers. The mountains saw thee, and writhed; the raging waters swept on; the deep gave forth its voice	The heavens dropped, yea, the clouds dropped water	Then the channels of the sea were seen
Thunder			The LORD also thundered in the heavens
Darkness	The sun and moon stood still in their habitation	——	He made darkness his covering around him, his canopy thick clouds dark with water
Arrows	At the light of thine arrows as they sped . . . flash . . . spear	——	He sent out his arrows . . . lightnings . . . blast
Before Yahweh (his wrath)	Thou didst bestride the earth in fury, thou didst trample the nations in anger. Thou didst trample the sea with thy horses	Before the LORD, before the LORD, the God of Israel	At thy rebuke, O Lord, at the blast of thy nostrils
God comes to help his people	Thou wentest forth for the salvation of thy people	(vs. 11) The triumphs of the LORD, the triumphs of his peasantry in Israel	He reached from on high, he took me, he drew me out of many waters.

"Great Lord, when thou goest forth in the bright heavens
. . .

Openest the great door of the bright heavens,
Then (Anu and) Enlil worship thee with joy . . ."

Stummer pointed out the similarity of this hymn's opening lines
to Judg. 5:4-5 (*op. cit.*, pp. 44 ff.). In another connection Gunkel
compared Ps. 68 and a hymn to Adad in Ungnad, *Die Religion
der Babylonier und Assyrer,* Jena, 1921, p. 194:

"When the Lord roars, the heavens tremble before him;
When Adad is angry, the earth quakes before him;
Great mountains break down before him . . ."

The clearly mythological language of the descriptions of epiphanies in the Psalms is to be explained on the basis of this background of other ancient religions. A whole list of parallels in individual features could be added.[45] Stummer, however, pointed
out[46] the characteristic difference between these and the biblical
epiphanies, that is, the Bible borrowed the schema, but the relation to the calendar has disappeared. In this connection it must
be said that in the place of a cosmic-mythical occurrence in the
Babylonian epiphanies there is in the O.T. a historical one:
Yahweh appears in order to help his people and to destroy his
foes. In one passage, however, this historicizing of a mythical
motif is carried one step further. In Ps. 114:1 the exodus of Israel
from Egypt has taken the place of God's appearing.[47] Ps. 114 is
the only one in which the epiphany constitutes the entire Psalm.[48]
It gives a late variation of the epiphany. Only with certain
reservations can Ps. 29 be included here. Here the epiphany
has been greatly modified in the direction of praise of the mighty

45. These are mentioned in part in the commentaries.
46. *Op. cit.*, p. 46.
47. Perhaps this alteration of the beginning of the Psalm can still be recognized.
Verse 2 begins, "Judah became his sanctuary." The suffix of the third person in the
two halves of vs. 2 (read, *memshalto*) can only refer to Yahweh. The subject of vs. 1,
however, is Israel. Verse 2 therefore presupposes a beginning of the Psalm in which
Yahweh was the subject! A similar change is to be assumed for Ps. 97, where the
original beginning of the epiphany was replaced by "The LORD reigns."
48. But LXX reads 114 and 115 as one Psalm.

voice of God, in a way that is similar to the hymn of the storm god Adad.[49]

In the other passages the epiphanies of God are encountered in a variety of contexts. The actual connection, however, remains always the same, whether explicit or implicit: God appears in order to help his people. The vitality of this motif which appears in the poetic literature of the O.T. in such varied places and at such different times is anchored in neither history nor cult, but in the experience of this help. And moreover in most of the epiphanies this event is related to the events that occurred at the beginning of Israel's history,[50] above all to the events at the Red Sea. This tight interweaving of the accounts of epiphanies with the initial events as well as the relatively independent appearance of the epiphanies in so many contexts can be explained most simply by the fact that the account of the epiphany was originally historicized in connection with those occurrences.[51]

That first occasion on which God came to the aid of his people was experienced anew in God's saving deeds. In this way it became a part of the songs of victory, and is heard again in a variety of contexts where God's helping and saving acts for his people are told or sung. In correspondence with later theology there also developed out of Yahweh's coming from a place in the desert a coming "from far" (Isa. 30:27), or "from the heavens" (Ps. 18:9), "out of his place" (Mic. 1:3), "out of Zion" (Ps. 50:2).

How greatly the epiphanies could be altered in this process is shown by the framework in Hab. 3 and Deut. 33. In the latter passage the epiphany is the framework of the blessing of Moses (vss. 2, 26 f.), and in Hab. 3 it is in the framework of the prophet's vision (vss. 2, 16).

In Isa. 30:27-33 and Mic. 1:3 ff. the epiphany is connected with the prophetic proclamation of doom. In Mic. 1:3 ff. the God who punishes strides forth against the capital city of his people (vss.

49. Jastrow, *Religion*, I, pp. 482 f. Cf. F. M. Cross, "Notes on a Canaanite Psalm in the O.T.," *BASOR* 117 (1950), pp. 19-21.
50. E.g., Judg. 5:4-5; Pss. 18:15; 77:15 f., 19 f., etc.
51. In this I am building on a surmise of Gunkel's in reference to Ps. 77:17-20: "May we assume that there was an old poem that expanded the saga of the Red Sea with such mythological features, and that this account contains echoes of it?"

6, 9), and in Isa. 30 God comes in order to intervene for his people against Assyria.

And finally in Zech. 9:14-17 and Isa. 59:15b-20 and 63:1-6 the epiphany is transformed into apocalypse. This line of development could be followed out even further.

The structure and motifs of the epiphany

A comparison of all the passages shows that *one* form is the basis of the many variants. There are only a few sentences that are met with only once, and several expressions are found in all the passages. The following three features are most frequently encountered, and they clearly represent the outline of the epiphany:

1. God's coming from, or his going forth from . . .
2. Cosmic disturbances which accompany this coming of God.
3. God's (wrathful) intervention for or against . . .

The difficulty of this outline lies in the fact that the third part is almost always demanded by the context and is to be deduced from it, but that it is hardly ever met with as a part of the epiphany. Thus for example in Judg. 5 and Ps. 18 the epiphany is separated from the account of victory, and in Deut. 33 the epiphany is the framework which contains the varied deeds of God for the various tribes. Even in Mic. 1:3 ff. God's intervention does not belong to the epiphany, but to the prophetic proclamation of doom which follows it. It is a part of the epiphany itself only in Hab. 3 and Isa. 30. On the other hand there are few epiphanies which do not contain allusions to the events of the early days. These facts strengthen the above surmise concerning the origin of the epiphany.

The explanation given here of the accounts of epiphanies in the Psalms differs radically from the cultic explanation of these passages as it has now been particularly developed by Weiser in the *Bertholet-Festschrift* (1950).[52]

52. "Zur Frage nach den Beziehungen der Psalmen zum Kult. Die Darstellung der Theophanie in den Psalmen und im Festkult," pp. 513-531.

1. Weiser rightly opposes the position that these passages are only poetic decorations, "stylized, obsolete traditional material." "For the poets of the Psalms the theophany must have still had living reality."

In his explanation Weiser proceeded from the thesis that "As far as the history of tradition is concerned the representations of the theophany have as their model the Sinai theophany." The careful comparison of Exod. 19 and Exod. 34 on the one hand with the epiphanies listed at the beginning of this section on the other hand gives the following results. The third of the three structural features which are encountered in almost all epiphanies is completely lacking in Exod. 19 and 34. Here God appears to a mediator in order to speak with him. What he says concerns of course the entire people, but the people take part in it only from afar. This self-revelation of God in Exod. 19 and 34 displays the basic features of a cultic occurrence:

> the locality: a specific place (the sacred boundary), 19:12, 13;
> the time: a specified day (with preparations for sanctification), 19:11;
> the personnel: Moses as the mediator of God's activity toward the people.

These cultic features are totally lacking in the epiphanies. They are in the nature of an event in history. We have then to distinguish between two types of divine appearances which are different from the very first.

In Exod. 19 and 34 God appears in order to reveal himself, and to communicate with his people through a mediator. This is a theophany.

In Judg. 5, etc., God appears in order to aid his people. This is an epiphany. (I am proposing this distinction of terminology on practical grounds.)

There are two groups of theophanies that may be distinguished from each other. In addition to the Sinai theophany there are later appearances of God to a prophet: 1 Kings 19; Isa. 6; Ezek. 1, 2. The significance of the divine appearance in these passages is to give a commission to the prophet (1 Kings 19:15) or to issue a call to prophetic service (Isa. 6; Ezek. 1, 2). They have the following points in common with the Sinai theophany:

I. God appears to one individual.
II. He appears in order to say something.

They are different in that the goal of God's appearing is in the latter cases the giving of a commission to a prophet (or the calling of a prophet), and thus they do not have the nature of a cultic occurrence.[53]

2. The distinction between two basic forms of God's appearing is therefore based on the different goals that these appearances have. But the actual events of God's appearing are different in the two instances.

(a) In Exod. 19 the report tells that God descended onto a mountain; in Judg. 5, etc., the report tells of God's breaking forth and coming out from a specific place.

(b) In Exod. 19 the fixed point, whose name we are told, is the *goal* of God's coming. In Judg. 5 the fixed point, whose name is given, is the *starting point* from which God comes.

(c) God himself determines the place at which he appears in Exod. 19, but in Judg. 5, the place where he appears is the scene of his people's distress.

3. The phenomena that accompany the two types of divine appearances are all that remains to them in common. But even here the agreement is by no means complete. In the epiphanies the accompanying phenomenon of Exod. 19 which is most often found is the quaking of the mountains. In Exod. 19, however, it is *the* mountain which quakes, and in the epiphanies we find only the plural (often with the parallelism of mountains and hills). The smoke, which is so important in the manifestation of God at Sinai, is found only once in the epiphanies, in Ps. 18. And here the conception is different from that in Exod. 19.

Of the various accompanying phenomena only the clouds cor-

53. Strictly speaking this is true only for 1 Kings 19 and Isa. 6. In Ezek. 1, 2, there are features which are unmistakably cultic.

respond exactly in the two types of passages. In Exod. 19 the quaking of the earth (the most frequent feature of the epiphanies) and the pouring of water from the clouds are both missing. In the account of the Yahwist[54] there is no shooting of arrows (lightning) and no divine thunder or voice. The Elohist speaks of lightning and of the blasts of a trumpet.

The total comparison shows that even with reference to the accompanying phenomena the differences are more pronounced than the similarities. Specifically, it appears that for the theophany in Exod. 19 the volcanic activity (fire, smoke, quaking of *one* mountain) are typical, and for the epiphanies, the meteorological activity (thunder, lightning, rain). In addition, however, we find the quaking of the earth and the shaking, or shattering, or melting of the mountains caused by the approach of Yahweh.

If this comparison of the two types of the manifestations of God is accurate, it will not be possible to call Exod. 19 the prototype of the epiphanies in the Psalter. This then casts doubt on the conclusion which Weiser drew from that thesis, namely that the theophany tradition had its origin in the cult of the festivals and that it went back to the Sinai theophany, which was "re-presented" and actualized in it. What Weiser said (*op. cit.*, p. 519) by way of summary concerning the significance of these theophanies, that God himself was hidden in the dark clouds and revealed himself in his word, fits only Exod. 19 and the prophetic revelations, and there is no single case where it applies to the epiphanies. Thus these epiphanies in the Psalms cannot bear witness to a "sacral act of sacramental effect," which presented a "cultic recapitulation of the ancient event" (that is, the theophany at Sinai).

The epiphanies belong to the context of the declarative praise of Israel. In them the God is praised who intervened in the decisive hour to help his people and to save them from their foes. They can be traced back to Israel's original experience of God's saving intervention at the Red Sea. This is shown by the allusions to this event in Hab. 3; Ps. 77; Nah. 1; Pss. 18; 114.

54. Following Beer's division of sources.

THE DECLARATIVE PSALM OF PRAISE OF THE INDIVIDUAL[55]

The structure can be seen in the chart. The Psalm of lament and the Psalm of praise of the individual are connected by three features.

I. In the "petition that has been heard" the vow of praise was followed by a section, usually consisting of only a single sentence, which corresponded in content and form to the main part of the declarative Psalm of praise: Pss. 13:5; 3:7; 10:17; 6:8; 54:7; 56:13; 31:7; 28:6; 31:21; 22:24, 31; Isa. 38:17b. All these statements are reports of deliverance. Ps. 56:13 reads, "For thou hast delivered my soul from death." *The petition that has been heard leads to declarative praise.*[56]

Here it at once becomes clear that (declarative) praise results from God's actions. God's intervention is the source of declarative praise. This declaration of praise reports what God has done. This is true both of the heard petition and of the declarative Psalm of praise.

II. The most frequent introduction in the declarative Psalms of praise is the voluntative, as in Ps. 30:1, "I will extol thee," perhaps also in Ps. 18:1 (cj.), in Ps. 138:1, 2a, "I give thee thanks, O LORD," in Ecclus. 51, and in Ps. 34:1, "I will bless the LORD at all times." In Ps. 107:8, 15, 21, 31, verbs in the jussive have the same force as the voluntative. This whole Psalm is no longer properly declarative praise, but a liturgical exhortation to such praise. The set formula, "O give thanks to the LORD, for he is good," has been placed at the beginning of the Psalm as an introduction to the liturgy.[57]

Precisely in this connection it becomes clear that the call to praise in the imperative is not the original introduction of the Psalm of declarative praise. Only once does an imperative serve

---

55. Pss. 116; 30; 40:1-12; 18; 107; 66:13-20; 118; 138; 34; 52; Jonah 2:2-9; Lam. 3:52-58; Job 33:26-28; Ecclus. 51; Ps. Sol. 15:1-6; 16:1-15 (Add. Dan. 1:65); Od. Sol. 25; 29 (9:2-11 is a mixed form). A unique development of the PI is found in Dan. 2:20-23 where declarative praise is introduced by descriptive praise.

56. So also Gunkel, *op. cit.,* p. 265.

57. Properly it is the introduction of the descriptive Psalm of praise, vss. 33-43, which concludes the whole Psalm.

Declarative Psalm of Praise (Psalm of Thanks) of the Individual

	Ps. 66:13-20	Ps. 30	Ps. 40	Ps. 18
Proclamation	(13-15) of sacrifice (16) of praise	I will extol thee, O LORD	(6-10)	I love thee (I will extol thee?), O LORD
Introductory summary	I cried aloud to him, and he was extolled with my tongue	For thou hast drawn me up	(11)	(3?)
Looking back at the time of need	If I had cherished iniquity in my heart	(6, 7) I said in my prosperity . . . Thou didst hide thy face		(4, 5) The cords of death encompassed me
Report of deliverance — I cried	(I cried aloud to him)	To thee, O LORD, I cried . . . Hear, O LORD	I waited patiently for the LORD	In my distress I called upon the LORD
Report of deliverance — He heard	But truly God has listened	—	He inclined to me and heard my cry	(6b) He heard (7-15, Epiphany)
Report of deliverance — He drew me out	(What he has done for me)	Thou hast turned for me my mourning into dancing	He drew me up . . . . and set my feet	16-19 He reached from on high, he took me

Renewed vow of praise	Blessed be God	That my soul may praise thee and not be silent. O LORD my God, I will give thanks to thee for ever	He put a new song in my mouth, a song of praise to our God	(49) For this I will extol thee, O LORD, among the nations
Praise (descriptive)	He has not rejected my prayer or removed his steadfast love from me	(The expansion in vss. 4-5)	(5) Thou hast multiplied ... thy wondrous deeds and thy thoughts toward us	(27) Thou dost deliver ... thou dost bring down (30 f.) This God— his way is perfect

as introduction of the PI, and this is in a declarative Psalm of praise that has become a liturgy, Ps. 118.[58]

The first part of Ps. 92, vss. 1-3, is a reflection on praise, and the introduction proper in vs. 4 is then also a voluntative. The same is true of Ps. 66, which begins with an exhortation to hear, as is usual in the wisdom literature.[59] Ps. 40A and Ps. Sol. 15 and 16 are without any introduction. Thus it can be said that the introduction of the declarative Psalms of praise is usually a voluntative. We saw that in its literary aspect the vow of praise is a conclusion, but in its content an announcement of the praise that was promised in the vow.[60] In the vow of praise, the Psalm of petition and lamentation is open toward praise. The voluntative, then, in the beginning of the declarative Psalm of praise, is simply taking up where the vow of praise left off. That which was promised there is now to take place.[61]

The change that was necessitated by the fact that the vow of praise at the end of the petition became the beginning of declarative praise was very slight. The vow of praise was made in the face of immediate, pressing need. Even when the one praying poured out his heart in the temple and received the answer through a saving word from God, he was alone in all this action. In the vow he promises to praise God, to make his name great. But this can happen only in a group of people (cf. the forensic aspects of the vow). The vow of praise therefore means in simple words that he will tell others what God has done for him. It is in this and not in the vocabulary of praise, not even in a simple

58. The same is true of the small declarative Psalm of praise, Add. Dan. 1:65, which is added to a descriptive Psalm of praise:
"Praise the Lord, O Hananiah, Azariah, and Mishael,
Sing his praise and magnify him forever,
For he has delivered us from the grave
And saved us from the power of death."
59. Similar to this is the exhortation to take heed to what was said at the end of Ps. 107 (vs. 43).
60. See above, pp. 38-39.
61. We have established that the same was true of the Babylonian psalms of praise. There, however, it is striking that the vow of praise soon lost its character of announcement of praise, and is to be found in many cases where it is followed directly by petition and lament. This must be connected with the fact that this announcement properly belongs to declarative praise. In Babylon, however, declarative praise of the individual did not develop into a separate category. We are aware of only the one example at the end of the lament of an old man. See above.

expression of thanks, that he praises God, that he extols him.

The only difference when the vow of praise is announced is that he *is* now in a group to whom he can tell what has happened to him. When this announcement comes at the beginning there are never specifications of a forensic nature. This would no longer have any meaning, because the forum, the group, the congregation is there. This is shown in Ps. 66:16. The use of the third person is grounded in this forensic nature of the praise of God. God is praised by the others who hear what he has done. But this does not mean that speaking of God in the third person is thereby any less praise that is directed to God.

III. The introductory summary. On several occasions in petitions that have been heard the vow of praise is based on a brief report, cf. especially Ps. 13:6. The declarative Psalm of praise of the individual (see the table) is the only Psalm category that regularly has after the introduction a short summary that corresponds exactly to the vow of praise and the reason it gives for praise:

> Ps. 116:1, "I love the Lord, because he has heard my voice and my supplications."
> Ps. 138:3, "On the day I called, thou didst answer me."

If the vow of praise of Ps. 56 is placed alongside the proclamation of Ps. 30, it can be seen how closely they correspond to each other:

> Ps. 56:12 f., "I will render thank offerings to thee. For thou hast delivered my soul from death."
> Ps. 30:1, 3, "I will extol thee, O Lord . . . thou hast brought up my soul from Sheol."

This third combining of petition and praise means that the two categories correspond in having a section that could exist in itself as a Psalm. It has exactly the same structure as Exod. 15:21!

What is the meaning of this short summary at the beginning

of the declarative Psalm of praise? The Psalms of praise of the people give a clue. We found in both Ps. 124 and Ps. 129 that they basically consist of a single sentence, or one compound sentence. The expansions through which this sentence became a song are recognizable as such at first glance. The Song of Miriam, Exod. 15:21, consists of only one sentence, and this is the case even with Ps. 93, if the introduction and conclusion are left out of account. The category of the declarative Psalm of praise clearly has the tendency to be concentrated in a single sentence. The content of this sentence is always the same (although it never becomes stereotyped, as should be noted especially here): God has intervened; he has saved. This, however, is never said as a statement of fact, but always as a confession. That is to say, the one who utters this sentence backs it up with his own existence; he is committed to the fact that this has happened to him. The principal word in the vocabulary of praise is *hōdāh*. The form of this word, "I will praise" (which is its most frequent form) means also "I will confess."

All true, living confession, however, occurs in *one* sentence.[62] The tendency of the declarative Psalm of praise to concentrate itself into *one* sentence, or the comprehension of the declarative Psalm of praise in a single sentence, is due to its being confession. In it God is lauded, praised, exalted by my acknowledging, confessing before men that he has helped me. As confession this praise of God must be capable of being comprehended in *one* sentence.

62. This is shown also by the history of the confessions of the church. The original confession of Christendom is the single sentence Κύριος Ιησους, (in various formulations, cf. esp. Phil. 2:11). The Apostles' Creed is a development of this sentence, which was then more and more expanded in the confessions of the great councils.
    The confessions of the Reformation period show this clearly once again. Luther's Smalcald Articles are in their structure clearly the development of *one* sentence (that of the *articulus stantis et cadentis ecclesiae*). The Augsburg Confession of Melanchthon is a summary of separate confessional sentences, but in it the one sentence of justification (Art. IV) is clearly the most prominent. That which then follows, the Apology and later the Formula of Concord, is no longer properly confession but explanation of confession. The moment of existence in which a confession can be made in one sentence was no longer present. In the Barmen Declaration this moment was again present, and all its statements are only the development of the first thesis, "Jesus Christ, as the holy Scriptures of the Old and New Testaments bear witness to him, is the *one* Word of God which we must hear, which we are to trust and obey in life and in death."

The fact that the Psalms of this category are still aware of the simplicity of true praise of God may be taken as a sign of the power of such simple confessional praise. Still more, however, must it be taken as a direct testimony to God's marvelous activity for mankind, testimony which preserved this simplicity despite the opposing tendency of all cultic activity. It is this simplicity which is seen in the words of the song of Exod. 15:21 and in the confession which defies reality in Ps. 126:3 and Job 1:21. However different these sentences and their circumstances may be, they still contain the same declaration, "Yahweh has acted." This means for the category of the declarative Psalms of praise of the individual that they are and intend to be nothing but the development of this one sentence. There is in the entire O.T. no finer and clearer example of such speaking that has no purpose except the explication of *one* sentence which precedes it. This is the reason that this group of Psalms has the strictest structure of all Psalm categories. There are in all 15 or 18 (Ps. 107 properly consists of four Psalms) songs which have this same structure. At least ten of them agree in the three parts and the four motifs of the main part, and almost all of them also agree in the order of the parts. This group enables us best to understand and demonstrate that the speech of the Psalms is determined from within. In spite of this regularity, the manner of speaking never becomes stereotyped. These Psalms show how a confession can speak with many voices and also with one.

The Main Section

In the Psalm of praise the various parts develop so obviously that there is no need to explain this further: the looking back to the time of need and the report proper of deliverance with its threefold message, "I cried to God—he heard—he delivered me." This then climaxes in a vow of praise that is usually followed by (in most cases descriptive) praise.

A few comments must be made on details.

1. The lament of the people and of the individual show the dual nature of the petitions "Hear!" and "Save!" The influence

of this duality was felt in the heard petitions, where praise resulted from the certainty of being heard. The report of God's intervention in declarative praise is likewise in two parts: he heard (inclined to me), and he delivered. Here that which we found to be the meaning of this duality of petition is confirmed. Neither in those petitions nor in this praise is it a question of only the momentary need and its being met. Suffering is understood in terms of God's being distant, asleep, or silent. Thus in the petition as in the praise it is really a question concerning God. It is a very serious matter that *God* should again be favorable to man. The Psalm of praise rejoices because *God* has heard and answered.

2. In the looking back to the time of need (this corresponds to the lament in the Psalms of petition) two features attract particular attention. This need may be described as being bound (Pss. 116:3; 18:4-5), but it is much more frequently described as being under the power of death.[63]

The typical speech of all these Psalms (including Jonah 2) makes it clear that the one speaking does not at all intend to speak of what actually happened to him. The Psalmist does not intend to relate what happened to him, but to testify what God has done for him. For the congregation before whom he praised God with this confession the important thing was not the "individual features" but the testimony of the witness. The one confessing in this manner did not intend to give a picture, but to call to them, "O magnify the LORD with me, and let us exalt his name together!" (Ps. 34:3).

3. Two statements seem to me to make it clear what it was that was decisive for the singers of these Psalms of praise.

(a) Ps. 40:2 f., "He drew me up from the desolate pit . . . He put a new song in my mouth, a song of praise to our God."

Here God's mighty deeds and the praise which grew out of them are viewed as one. It is a "new" song, not because of a new melody or new thoughts, but because God's miracle was new.

---

63. Cf. here Christoph Barth, *Die Errettung vom Tode*, Dissertation, Zollikon, 1947, I gratefully agree with all the essentials of this work.

(b) Ps: 30:11, "Thou hast turned for me my mourning into dancing."

The meaning of this sentence is similar to that of Ps. 40:3, but it speaks even more clearly of the transformation that has occurred in that the deliverance and the rejoicing that it produced are here totally united. In both passages praise is so closely and firmly related to God's saving intervention that it can even be designated as belonging itself to God's act of deliverance. These passages show better than any explanation the real Sitz-im-Leben of the praise of God in Israel (see above, p. 24).

4. What is the meaning of the vow of praise at the end of declarative praise, when it really belongs at the conclusion of petition? Psalm 116:12-14 gives a clue: "What shall I render to the LORD for all his bounty to me? I will lift up the cup of salvation . . ." This word is spoken at the end of declarative praise. And thus an "I will" stands at the end of almost each of these Psalms. Here again the inadequacy of the word "thank" is evident. What could be the significance of a vow of thanks at the end of a Psalm of thanks? If, however, these Psalms are a mode of praise, then the vow of praise at the end of declarative praise takes on special meaning in relation to the vow at the end of petition. That which the one praying promised at the end of petition, and proclaimed in the introduction of declarative praise, has now occurred. *But not a single one of these Psalms ends with the final part of the report, "and he drew me out."* That praise which arises out of the moment of deliverance does not come to an end when the deliverance has been reported once. Psalm 30:11 f., "Thou hast loosed my sackcloth and girded me with gladness, that my soul may praise thee and not be silent." In this sentence the meaning of the vow of praise at the end of the report of deliverance is clearly expressed: praise cannot be silent, but must be continually expressed. The same thing is said in a different manner in Ps. 118:17, "I shall not die, but I shall live, and recount the deeds of the LORD." The life which was restored by deliverance out of *sheōl* finds its meaning in praise.

Similarly Ps. 92:14 f., "They [the righteous] are ever full of sap and green, to show that the LORD is upright." Cf. Isa. 38:18 f.

5. A further distinction from the vow of praise at the end of the petition points in the same direction. While there the foundation of the vow of praise is in most passages the specific saving action, praise which summarizes, brings together, and describes always follows the vow of praise at the end of declarative praise, except in Ps. 66. Ps. 40:5 shows particularly well how this develops out of declarative praise: "Thou hast multiplied, O LORD my God, thy wondrous deeds." Here we can sense how declarative praise passes into descriptive praise. Similarly, Ps. 116:15, "Precious in the sight of the LORD is the death of his saints." This statement is still focused on specific deliverance, but it looks beyond one saving deed to the total activity of God.

Already at the end of the petitions that had been heard, statements which described the totality of God's actions, in Pss. 10:16, 18; 12:6; 102:24b-27 were made alongside the statement, "Yahweh has acted." They are the rule at the end of Psalms of declarative praise:

Jonah 2:9c, "Deliverance belongs to the LORD."
Ps. 18:25 f., "With the loyal thou dost show thyself loyal."
30, "This God—his way is perfect; the promise of the LORD proves true."
"He is a shield for all those who take refuge in him."
31, "For who is God, but the LORD?"
118:15 f., "The right hand of the LORD does valiantly, the right hand of the LORD is exalted."
138:5, "For great is the glory of the LORD."
8, "Thy steadfast love, O LORD, endures for ever."
34:7, "The angel of the LORD encamps around those who fear him, and delivers them."
34:22, "The LORD redeems the life of his servants; none of those who take refuge in him will be condemned."
92:15, "To show that the LORD is upright."
Job 33:26, "He recounts to men his salvation."

Ps. Sol. 15:1-3, "For thou art the hope and confidence of the poor."

Ps. Sol. 16:13-15, "For when thou dost not give strength."

6. An apparent variation in the sequence of parts is found in Ps. 30:4, 5:

"Sing praises to the LORD, O you his saints . . .
For his anger is but for a moment,
   and his favor is for a lifetime.
Weeping may tarry for the night,
   but joy comes with the morning."

These lines are to be compared with the previously cited passages Ps. 40:5 and Ps. 116:15. There is agreement as to the experience of the ones singing. But now it is said, "What happened to me is in accord with the manner in which Yahweh acts." This passage follows the introductory summary, and thus corresponds in content to the lines of descriptive praise which follow the report of deliverance. Here an imperative call to praise forms a new introduction for the statement. Ps. 30:1-5 is an illustration of the fact that declarative praise is introduced by a voluntative, and descriptive praise by an imperative.

7. The praise of the one who confesses before the congregation what God has done for him is always uttered with joy. We have here not a "cultic festive joy," as most interpreters say, but the joy of the one who has been saved. It is the joy of the one whom God has drawn up out of the dark depths, the joy of the one who has been freed from the "bands of death," the joy of the one in whose mouth God has placed a new song of praise to our God, of him whose sorrow God has turned into joy.

Ps. 92:4a, "For thou, O LORD, hast made me glad by thy work."

Ps. 107:29, "He made the storm be still. . . . Then they were glad." It is the joy of the sign of relief expressed in the cry *bārūk!* (see above), Ps. 66:19 f.: "But truly God has listened . . . Blessed be God, because he has not rejected my prayer or removed his steadfast love from me!"

THE FURTHER SIGNIFICANCE OF THE CATEGORY

1. Oriental parallels:

An Egyptian psalm: Roeder, *op. cit.*, pp. 52 ff., Erman, *op. cit.*, pp. 383 f., Gunkel, *op. cit.*, pp. 287 f.

Praise of Amon

Structure (following the numbers of the strophes in Gunkel):

1: Superscription: "Praise of Amon Re, the Lord of Karnak . . ."

2: Proclamation: "I write for him . . . I praise him . . . I proclaim his might . . ."

3: Exhortation to praise: "Beware of him—proclaim . . ."

4-5: Summation: "When I call upon thee, thou dost come to me to save me . . . It is thou who dost save the one who is in the underworld . . ."

6-7: Looking back to the time of trouble (indirect): "Neb-re, the painter of Amon . . . wrote songs of lament for him . . . on behalf of Nacht-Amon, who was sick and near death . . ."

8-9: Report of deliverance and praise of the deliverer.

10: Fulfillment of the vow of praise.

A Babylonian psalm: "Hiobpsalm," *ZiA*, p. 30 (Looking back to the time of need—I cried—he delivered).

Declarative praise of the people: *ZiA*, p. 7 (Hehn, no. 4).

Announcement: "I will glorify his deity, proclaim his might . . ."

Summary: "He . . . inclined his ear, showed grace."

There follows the report of deliverance: overthrow of the enemy, the Elamites.

2. In the Psalms of the O.T. it is still clearly recognizable that the declarative praise of the individual, like that of the people, is the development of *one* sentence. Among primitive peoples, declarative praise often consists of only this one sentence. Heiler (*op. cit.*, p. 95) gives the following examples:

Among the pygmies: "Waka, thou hast given me this buffalo, this honey!"

Konde: "Thou hast delivered me, O God!"

Jagga: "Thou, O God, hast enriched me with cattle, hast led me . . . !"

Ewe: "Thou hast delivered me out of this quarrel!"

Everywhere it is essentially the same sentence, with the same basic structure, "Thou, O God, hast done . . . ," which also forms the basis of the declarative praise of the O.T.

These examples, which could be multiplied, show that declarative praise is a basic mode of addressing God. They show also that this declarative praise is always present *before* that which is called "cult." In all these examples praise grows directly out of everyday experiences.

Heiler gives another example (*op. cit.*, p. 45) which leads a step further. "When the Herero encounter an unexpected good fortune, they stand still in astonishment, look up to heaven, and call out, 'Ndjambi Karunga!' " (the name of the god of heaven). This is thus an address of praise, which according to its significance is declarative praise. Here we have evidence of a very early stage, in which declarative and descriptive praise had not been yet distinguished. In this very simple calling on God[64] the meaning cannot be disputed from the context; this calling on God is declarative praise. Declarative praise is primary in relationship to descriptive praise.

3. It is not surprising that such a thing as declarative praise exists in many forms and in many places. Wherever a man encounters God's activity something like this must occur. It is astonishing, rather, that this category, insofar as I can see, is developed so richly and fully only in Israel. Nor is it here found isolated in the Psalms. The basic structure of this declarative praise: "Thou, O God, hast done . . ." occurs often and in many forms in the O.T. Here it will suffice to refer to only three examples, where a clear similarity is recognizable: Deut. 26:5-10, in the historical account of Ps. 106, and in the framework of the book of Judges.[65]

64. We still know this. Both the complaining petition and jubilant and thankful praise can be expressed by us too in moments when we are in the depths or the heights merely by calling out the name.

65. Von Rad (in *Das formgeschichtliche Problem des Hexateuch*, Stuttgart, 1938) designated Deut. 26:5-10 as a "small, historical Credo" and saw in it a primitive form of the transmission of the Pentateuch. If this "Credo" corresponds to the structure of the declarative Psalm of praise (cf. the table!), then we have here a connection that can hardly be disputed between the declarative Psalms of praise and the transmission of history in Israel at its roots.

	Deut. 26:5-10	Ps. 106	Judg. 2, 3
Looking back to the time of need	5, 6	6, 7	2:13-15; 3:7, 8
Then we cried	7a		
He heard their cry	7b	(44-46)	16a; 9a
He drew them out	10	8-11 (43a-46)	16b-18; 9b-11
Vow of praise and praise	8, 9	12	

The declarative Psalm of praise is found also in the N.T. The examples Luke 1:68-75 (declarative praise of the people) and 2:29-32 (1:46-55) (of the individual) show that declarative praise was again awakened when God performed the decisive, final deed of salvation for his people in the sending of his Son.[66]

But here a change occurs in declarative praise. The forensic element and the accompanying words of the vow of praise showed that confessional praise is at the same time proclamation: "I will tell of thy name to my brethren," Ps. 22:22. In declarative praise the one who has been saved declares God's great deeds. The messengers of Jesus Christ do the same thing, Acts 2:11. The difference is merely that God's saving, helping activity has now attained its τέλος in the sending of his Son. He has "fulfilled" the history of his people. In his resurrection the "pangs of death" (LXX) have been loosed, and it was to these that the one freed looked back in the declarative Psalms of praise.[67]

In the proclamation of the church of Jesus Christ the proclamation of declarative praise is continued and fulfilled. Thus it should not be surprising that the letter to the Romans, in which the message of the N.T. is summarized, has the structure of a declarative Psalm of praise.

In the history of the church of Jesus Christ the declarative Psalm of praise occurs once again in all clarity, in Luther's Reformation hymn.* The same resemblance is seen in the

66. Cf. Gunkel, *Harnack-Festschrift*, pp. 43 ff.
67. Acts 2:24 quotes the declarative Psalm of praise 18:5 = 116:3!
* "Dear Christians, One and All, Rejoice," No. 387 in *The Lutheran Hymnal*, Saint Louis: Concordia Publishing House, 1941.

fourth verse of the hymn "Sei Lob und Ehr' dem höchsten Gut
. . ." (Joh. Jak. Schütz) more briefly and almost in the exact
words of the Psalms, "I cried to the Lord in my need . . ."

	Romans	Dear Christians, One and All . . .
Proclamation	Rom. 1:14 f.	1: With holy rapture singing . . .
Summary	1:16 f.	Proclaim the wonders God hath done
Report of Deliverance		
1. Looking back to the time of need	1:18—3:20	2-3: Fast bound in Satan's chains I lay, Death brooded darkly o'er me . . .
2. I cried to Yahweh		4-5: But God beheld my wretched state Before the world's foundation . . .
3. He heard	3:21—8:39	6-9: The Son obeyed His Father's will . . . He came to be my Brother . . .
4. He drew me out		Life shall from death the victory win . . .
Vow of praise	12-15 "a living sacrifice" "your spiritual worship"	10: What I have done and taught, teach thou . . . So shall my kingdom flourish now and God be praised forever
Praise	16:25-27	

THE DESCRIPTIVE PSALM OF PRAISE

1. The Connections Between Declarative and Descriptive Praise.
1. It has been shown how the declarative Psalm of praise,

following the vow of praise, passes over into the descriptive Psalm of praise. Just as the conclusion of the petition that has been heard (vow of praise and summarizing report of deliverance) is a small but complete declarative Psalm of praise, so the conclusion of the declarative Psalm of praise is a descriptive Psalm of praise.

2. We found, in any case, clear traces of the introduction which is peculiar to descriptive praise: the call to praise in the imperative (esp. Ps. 30:4).

3. In addition there is in the content a yet firmer connection between the declarative and the descriptive Psalms of praise in a summarizing sentence which often occurs at the end of these songs:

Ps. 18:27, "For thou dost deliver . . . dost bring down."
Ps. 138:6, "The LORD is high, he regards the lowly."
Ps. 107:33-41, God humbles and exalts.
Ps. 118:22-23, "The stone which the builders rejected has become the head of the corner."
Job 5:11-14; Tobit 13:2.

In all these sentences the declaration of these Psalms is changed into description. For it was the theme of the declarative Psalms of praise that God looked down from his heights and rescued from the depths the one who called to him.

Strictly speaking this is said only in Ps. 138:6 and Ps. 118:22 f. The other passages add a complement, an expansion to this statement: there is a humbling that corresponds to this exaltation. What is the reason for this addition? In the Psalm of petition of the individual we found at the end, before the vow of praise, the formula of the double wish. Deliverance has here a twofold meaning for the one saved. In order that he may be freed, God's enemies must be destroyed or put to silence. Here the double praise of God, which looks in two directions, corresponds to this double wish. In Jonah 2:8-9 the double wish is included in the PI, and in Ps. 129:5-8 in the PP; in Ps. 34:10 and Ps. 107:42 it is included as a part of the expression of praise.

Ps. 34:10, "The young lions suffer want and hunger; but those who seek the LORD lack no good thing."[68] (Cf. Luke 1:53!)

> Ps. 107:42, "The upright see it and are glad; and all wickedness stops its mouth."
>
> Jonah 2:8 f., "Those who pay regard to vain idols forsake their true loyalty. But I with the voice of thanksgiving will sacrifice to thee."

It is certain, however, that originally there was nothing but the simple sentence which looked only at the miracle of exaltation. This sentence is the basic theme of the descriptive Psalm of praise. This is shown with special clarity in Ps. 113.

> 1-3, Call to praise
> 4-5, God is exalted (read 6b after 5a)
> 5b and 6a, He who is enthroned on high—he who looks into the depth
> 7-9, God exalts the lowly
> 5b and 6a constitute the midpoint of the Psalm; 5b summarizes 4-5, and 6a is developed in 7-9.

The Psalm has a very simple and clear structure. The language is obviously different from that of the declarative Psalms of praise. It is speech directed toward God in the sense that it looks away from the unique occurrence of a specific deliverance and speaks of God's majesty and grace in a summarizing, recapitulating, and descriptive manner. But in Israel this recapitulating praise which brings together descriptions never lost its connection with the unique, concrete intervention which was experienced in the history of the people or of the individual. In Ps. 113 a single sentence stands at the midpoint, vss. 5b and 6a. Here there is brought together in a general statement that which was reported as a specific experience of deliverance. This is what the one who cried out of the depths was pleading for: Look! Come down! Hear! This is what the one delivered told to others:

68. The author reads "the rich" for "the young lions," following the LXX.

Ps. 40:1, "He inclined to me and heard my cry."

Just as there the action which had been experienced by the one giving praise was at first summarized in *one* sentence, so here it is stated in *one* sentence who the God is or what he is like, whom we are called to praise in the Psalm.[69]

Verses 7-9 explain what it means for those who are in the depths when God looks down to them from the heights. It means a reversal of fortune, a "joyous change." This change is described in a twofold action: God elevates the poor man out of the depths and gives him a new, good place. The "drawing up" is the fourth motif of the "report of deliverance" in the declarative Psalms of praise. There is added an element which was not mentioned or was only implied in the declarative Psalms of praise, the new, transformed situation of good fortune, of salvation for the one who has been delivered; this is the "life" for which he prayed. The laments almost always dwelt on the shame which the isolation of grief brought with it. Suffering was consistently viewed in its social aspects. Everyone forsook the sufferer; they fled from him as from a leper; they pointed their fingers at him and said that God had forsaken him. This was the depth of suffering and the real sharpness of the trial. In Ps. 113 this suffering is transformed: the one who is saved regains his honor in the sight of others. There is included in the raising of the poor from the dust that which we would term the real deliverance, whether that is the healing of sickness, or justification before one's enemies, or deliverance from the danger of death. These, however, are not described, but only the social significance of the deliverance.

In vs. 8 and vs. 9 two important examples of the restoration of honor are described: the example of the childless woman, which is found so often in the O.T., and the restoration of the honor of a man in his clan.

The fact that Ps. 113 has as its center and then develops a single sentence which describes and summarizes what is reported in the declarative Psalms of praise can be demonstrated once

---

69. Cf. Isa. 63. See above, pp. 47 ff.

more by the singular structure of the Psalm. The declarative sentence in vss. 4-5 tells of the glory of God, but it is the participles in 5b and 6a, and not this sentence, which form the central part of the Psalm. These participles, which make the declaration more specific, speak of precisely the other element: that he descends from that height to our depths. The only significance which the majesty of God has for the one giving praise here is that it comes down to where we are.

In this basic form of the descriptive Psalm of praise we can see the line along which the O.T. moves in all decisive passages when it speaks of God. God is the one whom Israel encountered in its history, and whom it experienced as the one who from his heights intervenes in the depths of tribulation.[70]

The close relationship of Ps. 113 to the declarative Psalms of praise can be noted in yet another of its distinctive modes of expression. The Psalm does not contain a single noun descriptive of God. Such nouns, which we usually call the attributes of God, are otherwise quite characteristic of descriptive praise. That which is described in Ps. 113:6-8 is called in precisely comparable contexts (cf. the table) at the same position in the Psalm *hesed* (i.e., "grace"). Here reference should be made to the results of the work of N. Glueck, *Das Wort hesed in alttestamentlichen Sprachgebrauch als menschliche und göttliche gemeinschaftsgemässe Verhaltungsweise.*[71] Here it is shown that on the basis of the usage in the O.T. our category of "attribute" is not relevant. A specific mode of relationship always precedes the occurrence of *hesed.* "Only those who stand in a specific relationship to one another receive and express *hesed*" (*op. cit.,* p. 3). "*Hesed* is a mode of relationship that corresponds to the relationship of law and duty" (*ibid.,* p. 20). "The *hesed* of God is to be understood only as the way in which God stands in a communal relationship to those who belong to him. . . . God's *hesed*

70. It is thus not accidental that this same declaration is found also in the sermon in Deuteronomy: Deut. 10:14, "Behold, to the LORD your God belong heaven and the heaven of heavens, the earth with all that is in it"; 15, "yet the LORD set his heart in love upon your fathers and chose their descendents after them, you above all peoples."
71. Giessen, 1927.

is the consequence of his covenant, or of his promise, or of his oath" (*ibid.*, p. 65)[72]

Hesed is thus a way in which God is related in a community. Precisely in this is it grace in the proper sense of the word. The O.T. does not know any grace except this. God's grace is both a free expression and a relationship determined by a community. It never becomes God's "duty," but it also never was and never is merely arbitrary. Freedom and restriction are one in God's grace.

Psalm 113 describes God's *hesed*. It is the other side of his majesty; it is the looking into the depths by the one who is enthroned in the heights. That is the constantly recurring declaration of the descriptive Psalms of praise.[73]

This can be made clear by reference to Ps. 107. This is a liturgical combination of four PI. It is no longer the individual who speaks, but individuals are called upon to praise God for the deliverance which they have experienced. The first of these reports concludes with the words: "Let them thank the LORD for his steadfast love [*hesed*], for his wonderful works to the sons of men" (vss. 8, 15, 21, 31). This sentence recurs after each of the reports. In this occurrence those whom Yahweh has saved encounter God's *hesed*. All four accounts are concerned with everyday occurrences, everyday reality in all its manifold fullness. The merchant or the wanderer on his way through the wilderness, the prisoner who is paying for his crime, the sick, the seafarers, have all experienced God's *hesed* in their own particular existence. They cry to him from *their* depths and he looks down into *their* depths. In this they experience God's *hesed*. That is to say, God's *hesed* is expressed each time he looks down into the depths of a specific need (that of the people or that of an individual); it is the mode of relationship to God which is experienced when one is "drawn out." The fact that

72. There is a more recent investigation of the concept *hesed* in N. H. Snaith, *The Distinctive Ideas of the O.T.*, London, 1944, pp. 94-130.

73. It will perhaps become clearer that the Psalms say this again and again by comparison with a sentence from a novel of the period after the First World War, *Mich Hungert* by Georg Fink, Berlin, 1926, on the next to last page: "No God descends into the abysses of his creation."

the one delivered experiences God's grace is substantiated by Ps. 116:5, "Gracious [*hannun*] is the LORD, and righteous; our God is merciful." Ps. 18:50, "and shows steadfast love [*hesed*] to his anointed." Ps. 66:20, "Blessed be God, because he has not . . . removed his steadfast love [*hesed*] from me!" Pss. 118:1 (=107:1); 138:2; 92:2. Cf. Ps. 40:10 f.

It is thus the intention of all these Psalms to tell of God's grace (even those which do not contain the word, as Ps. 30). Everywhere we encounter Yahweh's true grace in a unique intervention, and, as has been shown in relation to Ps. 107, it means deliverance in time of need. There is nothing else that can be meant by the *hesed* of God which is praised in the descriptive Psalms of praise. Ps. 107:1 and Ps. 118:1 mean the same thing as the sentence in Ps. 136:1. Even in the descriptive Psalms of praise God is not praised as "God in himself," as one transcendentally present, as a "being" with "attributes," but as the same God whose actions were reported in the declarative Psalms of praise. The fact that all these Psalms speak only in praise and in calling to such praise and never in a manner of attempting to establish the fact that something is there agrees with this view. Praise is response to God's actions. God's majesty and goodness can be spoken of only in such a response. This can be shown by the structure of the descriptive Psalm of praise.

2. The Structure of the Descriptive Psalm of Praise

The descriptive Psalms of praise do not have the same unity of structure as the declarative. Nevertheless they are clearly distinguished from the sections of praise in the Babylonian and the Egyptian psalms in that they (1) have a fixed, well-defined basic structure, and (2) do not consist of a summation of predicates and declarations of praise, but like Ps. 113, whether more or less clearly, are the development and expansion of a single declaration, the one which so clearly forms the center of Ps. 113.

The first group consists of Pss. 113; 117; 33; 36; 105; 135; 136; 147; 146; 111; 89:5-18; Neh. 9:6-31; 1 Sam. 2:1-10; Nah. 1:2-11 (without an imperative); cf. Jer. 32:17-23.

1. All these Psalms begin with an imperative call to praise. This confirms that the imperative call to praise is an integral part of descriptive praise. In Ps. 65 its place has been taken by a reflection on praise (as Ps. 92, cf. 33:1; 147). In Ps. 146, where the transition to a didactic Psalm can be noted, the call to praise is issued in the proper place. The most frequent verb is *hillēl:* Pss. 113; 117; 135; 147; 146; noun form in Ps. 65. *Hōdāh* occurs only in Ps. 136, and accompanying words of praise are found in Ps. 147 (3 terms); Ps. 33 (6); Ps. 105 (9!).[74]

2. In most of the Psalms there follows the reason for praise, which is also an introductory summary, corresponding to the declarative Psalms of praise. This introductory summary, even though it is not found in all the Psalms, is the surest sign that what is said in these Psalms is not synthetic but analytic, that is, we do not have sentences heaped on one another, but *one* sentence is developed.

Ps. 117[75] consists of only the one sentence which gives the reason for the imperative of the first verse, "For great is [=he has made] his steadfast love toward us; and the faithfulness of the LORD endures for ever." The first part of the sentence clearly contains the two motifs of Ps. 113, Yahweh's might over us, and the reality of the steadfast love and faithfulness which are ever available for us through his power. These two statements, which praise God's majesty and his condescension to us, run through all these Psalms without exception. They are, however, not always summarized in advance. This is the case in the following Psalms:

Ps. 136:1, "For he is good, for his steadfast love endures for ever."

2 f., "God of gods, ... Lord of lords."

Ps. 135:3 f., "For the LORD is good; ... the LORD has chosen Jacob for himself."

74. In Neh. 9:5 ff. the original situation of this imperative call to praise is related. Originally it was not a part of the Psalm, but preceded it: "Then the Levites . . . said, 'Stand up and bless the LORD your God . . .'" There follows a long Psalm of praise which extends to the end of the chapter.

75. This is probably the conclusion of a small collection of Psalms.

5, "The LORD is great."

Ps. 33:5, "He loves righteousness and justice; the earth is
full of the steadfast love of the LORD."

In the following Psalms there is no clear division in the transition to the main part of the Psalm:

Ps. 105:7, "His judgments are in all the earth."
8, "He is mindful of his covenant for ever."
Ps. 147:2-3, the one who heals; 3-4, the Creator, the Lord.
Ps. 146, an entirely different introduction, with a transition
to exhortation and instruction, vss. 3-5.

There is also in addition to this another pair of terms: God
exalts and brings low. Ps. 147:6; 1 Sam. 2:4-8 (compare the passages in the declarative Psalms of praise, above, pp. 41-42).[76]
This sentence, "God exalts and brings low," as a summary of
descriptive praise, shows from another side that in such praise
it is not an existent, available God who is praised, but the One
who intervenes in history. Israel's historical experience stands
behind this sentence. It demonstrates once again a connection
between the historical writings and the Psalms. In the former
it is a constant motif that an insignificant person is chosen by
Yahweh and thereby exalted, that Yahweh does not perform his
mighty deeds for his people through the great, the famous, the
daring, but through small, limited, despised men. *This* is the
God who is praised here. This sentence, however, includes the
whole nation as well as the individual; the God who is praised
is the one who can reverse the destiny of his people, who has
destroyed and will destroy great and powerful nations. This
sentence can also be heard behind the strong hope of Israel in
the hardest times, for Israel knows that God exalts and brings
low. But that it also held good for the individual and was so
understood by him is shown especially by 1 Sam. 2. Here is the
strongest expression of exalting and bringing low: vs. 6, "The

76. Outside of this group there are also Tobit 13:2; Ecclus. 10:14-17; Luke 1:51-53;
Pss. 107:39-41; 68:6; 75:7 (Deut. 32:43); 1 Chron. 29:12b (only exaltation); Ps.
Sol. 2:31.

LORD kills and brings to life; he brings down to Sheol and raises up." Its reappearance in Luke 1 indicates how strong this motif was.

This motif alone is enough to show that even in descriptive praise we are dealing with a God who comes down into our history, and not with one who is contemplated in a speculative manner. 1 Sam. 2:6 shows clearly that behind this motif there stands the confession of praise of the one who has been saved, as found in the declarative Psalm of praise.

3. This double sentence of God's actions from the heights into the depths, or of his majesty and his grace is now further developed and supplemented. This can be shown first of all in Ps. 33:

> vss. 1-3, A call to praise in the imperative.
> 4 then, "The word of the LORD is upright; and all his work is done in faithfulness" (=vss. 5-19).
> 5, "He loves righteousness and justice; the earth is full of the steadfast love of the LORD."
> 5a ⌈ 6-9, the Creator: "By the word of the LORD the heavens were made."
> ⌈└ 10-12, The Lord of history: "The Lord brings the counsel of the nations to nought."
> 5b │ 13-19, "The LORD looks down from heaven . . . on those who fear him."
> └ 16-17, Human power is of no avail!
> 20-21, Confession of confidence: "He is our help."
> 22, *Petition:* "Let thy steadfast love, O LORD, be upon us."

The structure of this Psalm shows with all clarity that it is really the development of the two sentences, vs. 4 and vs. 5.[77]

The greatness of Yahweh and his majesty are not expressed in any specific term. Thus the account of creation in vss. 6-9

---

77. Gunkel on the structure of this Psalm: "Where so much value is given to the number of the lines (alphabetical principle: the number of verses corresponds to the number of letters) it is understandable that the order of thoughts is not particularly strict and that the separate groups of thoughts stand in comparative independence of one another . . . Therefore the exegetes disagree about the divisions of the Psalm."

proclaims his greatness all the more clearly, and at its end all the world is called to fear him whose word established the world. The development of the one part of the theme sentence in the descriptive Psalm of praise has the meaning of exalting. Here the basic statement is developed *in order that* Yahweh may be feared. This speaking of God the Creator is completely directed toward God, and does not intend to unfold the greatness of Yahweh in the sense of an explanation that is directed to man. It arises, not from any theoretical interest, but from the will to praise him. Creation is here the secondary theme. It is the creation that is spoken of for the sake of the Creator, and not the Creator for the sake of the creation.[78]

4. The praise of the Creator in the other Psalms of the category.

Ps. 136:5, "who by understanding made the heavens, for his steadfast love endures for ever."

6, "who spread out the earth upon the waters, for his steadfast love endures for ever."

7-9, "who made the great lights . . . sun . . . moon . . . for his steadfast love endures for ever."

78. At this point the work of von Rad, "Das theologische Problem des alttestamentlichen Schöpfungsglaubens," *Werden und Wesen des A.T.*, Berlin, 1936, pp. 138 ff., can be substantiated and carried a step further. What von Rad says of Second Isaiah, "The creation faith is never the main theme of a passage—it is never adduced for its own sake," p. 140, holds also for the descriptive Psalms of praise. In the structure of these Psalms we can see the preliminary step that led to Second Isaiah, where it is only formulated more clearly, but is not new, namely that "the protological is brought together with the soteriological." In these Psalms praise of the Creator is development of the twofold sentence of Yahweh's majesty and grace, in which that which the declarative Psalms report is described and summarized, and this is the soteriological element. Here too the exaltation of Yahweh experienced by the one saved is the basis of the praise of the Creator, even though not explicitly so. It is the development of the praise of the one who exalts and brings low. Von Rad's thesis (p. 143) that the soteriological understanding of the work of creation is the basic expression of the Yahweh religion concerning Yahweh the Creator of the world is further attested by the structure of the descriptive Psalms of praise. The relationship of the descriptive Psalm of praise to the declarative shows that the statements about creation are secondary with respect to those of Yahweh's intervention to save. In them a statement of the declarative Psalm of praise is developed. This does not mean that all declarative Psalms must be older than all descriptive ones. The category of the declarative Psalm of praise must, however, be given precedence over that of the descriptive. The latter can be explained only in terms of the former, and some of the declarative Psalms show how the descriptive Psalm of praise developed out of them. In this connection compare the almost total absence of declarative Psalms of praise in Babylon, see above p. 36.

10, "who smote the first-born of Egypt."[79]

In most of the Psalms of the group the praise of the Creator passes directly into praise of the Lord of history.[80]

God's activity in the creation and direction of his works is the same as his activity in the history of the nations. What is created and what occurs have not yet been separated from one another; the special realm "nature" does not yet exist. Yahweh's lordship is praised in both. Thus historical occurrences can frequently be spoken of in mythical pictures, which generally have also a cosmic significance.[81]

This praise of the Lord of history stands quite properly in the center between the praise of the majesty of God and the praise of his grace. His Lordship over the history of all nations witnesses to his majesty, but usually Yahweh's mighty actions in history which bring help to his people are the ones which are described. This is the significance of the motif, Ps. 33:10 f. "The LORD brings the counsel of the nations to nought." In Ps. 136:10-22 it is only the saving activity of Yahweh that is described. In Ps. 65:7 God's activity in creation and in history are spoken of in the same sentence, "who dost still the roaring of the seas, . . . the tumult of the peoples." Psalm 135:8-12 corresponds to Ps. 136. Psalm 105:7, 1 Sam. 2:10, and Ps. 89:13 f. correspond rather to Ps. 33. In Ps. 147 and Neh. 9 praise of the Lord of history is only indirectly present; Ps. 147:2, 13a, 14a, in the protection of Jerusalem from her foes; in Neh. 9, in the great historical account in vss. 9-31. It is changed distinctively in Ps. 146:3-5.[82]

---

79. Except for Ps. 105 all Psalms of this group contain praise of the Creator: Pss. 65:6-8; 135:6-7; 147:4, 8, 16-18; 146:6; 1 Sam. 2:8c; Ps. 89:9-12; Neh. 9:6b. In addition, Pss. 24:1-2; 90:2-5; Judith 16:15; Job 9:5-10; Pr. Man. 2; Ecclus. 39:16 ff.; Od. Sol. 16:10-19.

80. Cf. H. Schmidt's commentary in *HAT*, on Ps. 29, p. 54: "It is peculiar to the hymns that in them praise customarily directs its attention to two things, first to God's powerful activity in nature, in creation, and then to his work in the history of his people."

81. In the following passages it is expressed especially clearly that God is praised as both Creator and Lord of history: Isa. 40:12-31; 43:1-7, 14-15, 16-20; 44:24-28; 45:1-7, etc.

82. Praise of the Lord of history is also found in Job 12:14-25. It corresponds to the praise of the Creator in the preceding speech of Job in 9:5-10. The same elements are together in Ps. Sol. 2:29b-31 and 34-37.

5. Praise of the Lord of history can pass immediately into praise of his grace.

> Ps. 33:13, "The LORD looks down from heaven."
>   18, "Behold, the eye of the LORD is on those who fear him."
>   19, "That he may deliver their soul from death."

The same "looking into the depths" occurs, in addition to Ps. 113 and Ps. 33, in other Psalms, widely removed from them in time:

Add. Dan. 1:32, "Blessed art thou, who enthroned on the Cherubim lookest into the depths."

Luke 1:48, "For he has regarded the low estate of his handmaiden."

This remained the living source of praise from the earliest beginnings of Israel's history to the commencement of the new age: the joyous experience that God looks into the depths and saves from the depths. Not only the declarative Psalms of praise, but also the descriptive bear witness to this. Many passages are similar in this respect.

> Ps. 136:23 f., "It is he who remembered us in our low estate . . . and rescued us from our foes."
>
> Ps. 135:14, "For the LORD will vindicate his people, and have compassion on his servants."
>
> Ps. 105:8-11, "He is mindful of his covenant."
>   vss. 12-44, He helped his people. Cf. Neh. 9:9-31.
>
> Ps. 147:2-3, "The LORD builds up Jerusalem; . . . He heals the brokenhearted."
>   vs. 6, "The LORD lifts up the downtrodden."
>   vss. 15, 19, 20, "He declares his word to Jacob."
>
> Ps. 65:2, 3b, "O thou who hearest prayer . . . thou dost forgive."
>
> Ps. 146:7, "Who executes judgment for the oppressed; who gives food to the hungry" (cf. vss. 8-9).

Ps. 89:17b, "By thy favor our horn is exalted" (cf. vss. 14-18, 1 Sam. 2:9).[83]
It is to be noted that in this second section, in which Yahweh's grace is described, it is always expressed by the use of verbs (including several very late passages). Where God's grace is praised, there his actions are praised.

6. We noted earlier that there was a tendency to supplement the descriptive Psalms of praise in two places. In one, the statement of exaltation from the depths, which summarizes declarative praise (Ps. 113:7-9), was supplemented by the statement concerning bringing down the high and the mighty. But then the double statement of Yahweh's majesty and grace, which forms the basis of descriptive praise, is also to be understood as such a supplement. In the declarative Psalms of praise it is implicit in the motif, "He drew . . . out of the depths." This can be done only from on high. This fact that Yahweh is on high became as such the theme of the descriptive Psalms of praise. In addition there is also a third supplement: Yahweh's looking down into the depths means not only deliverance, but also *preservation*. In the declarative Psalms of praise, preservation and support (that is, continuity of action) are seldom mentioned. They appear marginally in Ps. 107:9. When a Psalm culminates in a petition, this is a petition for continuous action, Pss. 138:8; 33:22.

In the descriptive Psalms of praise, the praise of the one who upholds and preserves appears alongside the praise of the one who saves. This motif is occasionally encountered in the praise of the Creator, who in certain Psalms is praised also as the Preserver, Ps. 147:8, 9, 13, 14; Neh. 9:6c; Ps. 36:6b-9, and especially Ps. 65:9-13. It becomes the only theme in Ecclus. 39:14b-35.

But the preserving love of God occupies also another place in descriptive praise. In a number of Psalms God's saving action is directly combined with a specific kind of preservation, preservation from hunger. This is seen especially in the following:

83. In addition, Ps. 68:5a, 8, 12; Nah. 1:7-8; Pr. of Man. 6-7; 2 Chron. 6:14 f.; Ezra 3:11; Neh. 1:5; Luke 1:48, 50, 54, 55; 2:14b; Ecclus. 15:19.

Ps. 136:23, "who remembered us in our low estate."
    24, "and rescued us from our foes."
    25, "he who gives food to all flesh."

Ps. 33:19, "that he may deliver their soul from death, and keep them alive in famine."

Ps. 111:5, "He provides food for those who fear him; he is ever mindful of his covenant."

Ps. 145:14 f., "The LORD upholds all who are falling, and raises up all who are bowed down. The eyes of all look to thee, and thou givest them their food in due season." Cf. Ps. 104:10-30.

7. This Psalm category does not have a concluding formula. Most of these Psalms end with the praise of the goodness of God without any set form of ending. Psalm 33 has a confession of confidence in vss. 20 f., but then concludes in vs. 22 with a petition. In some Psalms of this group the imperative at the beginning of the Psalm is repeated: Ps. 136; Ps. 135; Tobit 13:6-8 (imperative, voluntative, and jussive!). In two there is an exhortation at the end, Ps. 65 and Ps. 105. One ends with a word of wisdom, Ps. 111. It is clear, however, that the original structure had an imperative call to praise only at the beginning; the expansion in praise of the statement of God's majesty and goodness followed. These are the two parts of the descriptive Psalm of praise.

This group is clearly recognizable as a further development of the simple form of the category. In the indicative statements, praise proper, it agrees with the preceding group. The further development consists in the insertion of a new imperative between the two basic statements, "Yahweh is exalted—Yahweh is good," and, in a few of the Psalms, in the occurrence of the imperative once again at the end. It is clearly a development that was determined liturgically and designed for liturgical use, and as a result of this the imperatives came to outnumber completely the proper exclamations of praise in these Psalms.

The insertion of the imperatives between the two parts of

3. The Imperative Psalms[84]

	Imperative call to praise	God's majesty	Imperative call to praise	God's goodness
100	Make a joyful noise to the LORD, all the lands!	Know that the LORD is God! It is he that made us	Enter . . . his courts with praise!	For the LORD is good; his steadfast love endures for ever
95	O come, let us sing to the LORD	For the LORD is a great God (4-5, the earth is his)	O come, let us worship and bow down	For he is our God, and we are the people of his pasture (in 7b-11 a prophetic exhortation follows)
148	Praise the LORD from the heavens . . . Praise the LORD from the earth	For he commanded and they were created . . . For his name alone is exalted	(Praise is proper to all his saints)	14, He has raised up a horn for his people
145	I will extol thee, my God and King	(God is great and greatly to be praised, vss. 13-20)	6-7, Men shall proclaim the might of thy terrible acts . . . They shall pour forth the fame of thy abundant goodness	8-9, The LORD is gracious and merciful (13-20 passim) 21, an exhortation to praise
150	Praise God in . . .	. . . for his mighty deeds . . . according to his exceeding greatness	Praise him with . . . Let everything that breathes praise the LORD!	———

84. Pss. 100; 148; 150; 145; 95A; Add. Dan. 1:29 ff.

the main section confirms the structure which was demonstrated for the first group. Aside from the increase in the number of imperatives this group scarcely presents any new elements.

1. Introduction. Imperative in Pss. 100; 148; 150; Add. Dan. 1. In Ps. 95 there is a cohortative instead of the imperative and in Ps. 145 voluntative and jussive forms alternate throughout the Psalm. Ps. 150 consists solely of manifold variations of the imperative call to praise.

2. Main section. With the exception of Ps. 150, where the praise of the grace of God has given way before the impressive imperatives, all these Psalms contain the praise of God in his majesty and in his goodness. Ps. 148 departs from this to the extent that the main section is not divided according to what is to be praised in God, but according to the subjects who are called to praise: vss. 1-6, "Praise the LORD from the heaven," vss. 7-12, "Praise the LORD from the earth." The two statements of the main section are scarcely developed in any of these Psalms. It is characteristic that the Creator is praised, but not the Lord of history. The fact that in the second part static declarations take the place of active ones corresponds to this. The more strongly liturgical the style becomes, the more static the praise is!

It can be stated with certainty that this group, in relation to the first group, constitutes a further development. The opposite relation seems to me to be impossible. The direction of this development is shown clearly by what is probably the latest Psalm of the group, Add. Dan. 1:29 ff. The imperative conclusions of the Psalms (especially Ps. 103), the imperative framework, and the conclusions of the books of the Psalter all point in the same direction.[85]

85. Gunkel held that the imperative call to praise, the "Hallelujah," was the "basic unit of hymn singing" (*Einleitung*, p. 37 f. and the article "Halleluja" in *RGG*[2]. So also Hempel, *Literaturgeschichte*, p. 19). Nöldeke expressly opposed this in the *Baudissin-Festschrift*, pp. 375-380, as Delitzsch had done much earlier in his commentary on Ps. 104:35 (p. 689). So also Greiff, *Das Gebet im A.T.*, 1915, p. 76. On the basis of a total investigation of the verbs and forms of the praise of God it can be concluded with certainty that Gunkel's thesis cannot be maintained. Nor is it correct that "originally at the end of a song of praise all the people joined in" (p. 37), for it is an exhortation to praise and therefore belongs *before* the song of praise proper (this is shown, e.g., by Neh. 9:5 ff.). This exhortation to praise was then united to the song of praise itself and thus became the in-

4. Conclusion of Groups 2 and 3

All the sentences in which God is here praised have their individual parallels in the Babylonian, Egyptian, and many other psalms. If the essential element in the Psalms were the "thoughts about God" which are expressed here, then in this category a clear and significant difference could scarcely be shown between biblical Psalms and the others. As far as the thought is concerned it would not be particularly difficult to reduce descriptive praise in the Babylonian psalms, for instance, to this twofold denominator of majesty and grace. And further, it is of the nature of descriptive praise that it does not have the strict structure of declarative praise. Here as elsewhere descriptive praise flows and overflows. Expression is here restricted the least.

When this has been granted, we then see in the proper light what it means that in this category of the Psalms of the O.T. a structure can nevertheless be recognized, a structure in which the following traits are evident:

1. All these Psalms still show that they do not speak by way of summary but by unfolding. There is not a one of the descriptive Psalms of praise which is a summation of predications of praise (which are as good as nonexistent) or of declarations of praise. *All* descriptive Psalms of praise are—more or less clearly —governed by the tension of the relation to each other of the two statements that God is enthroned in majesty, and *yet* is the one who is moved with compassion.[86]

Through this dominant motif it becomes clear that descriptive praise lives on declarative praise. In this one statement, which stands in the middle of these Psalms, that which is reported in the declarative Psalms of praise is described by way of summary.[87]

---

troduction of the descriptive Psalm of praise. Through the tendency to construct a framework it then also became a concluding formula. Only in the final stage did it become fully separated from the Psalm and become the independent "Hallelujah," existing in and for itself.

86. It is possible that this basic structure of descriptive praise is repeated in the prologue of John's Gospel in the relationship of its two parts, vss. 1-13 and 14-18, to each other. In any case, vs. 14 corresponds exactly to the motif of praise that God looks out of his heights into our depths in order to help those in the depths.

87. Corresponding to this, in John 1:14-16 descriptive praise is combined with the

2. The "exegetical speaking" of the descriptive Psalm of praise becomes evident in a large number of Psalms, in that the one twofold statement is developed in specific declarations which agree in a whole group of Psalms even in their order, and whose individual motifs are repeated in many others. God's greatness, his exaltation, his majesty are seen in creation and in his Lordship in history.

God's grace is at work when he looks into the depths, saves, redeems, and heals, and "exalts the horn of his people." But it is also at work there where he sustains his creation and gives bread to the hungry.

3. In the structure of these Psalms a tendency to praise God's deity in its fullness can be noticed. That is the tendency which forms the basis for this category. It is demonstrated in a threefold expansion: 1. the one who looks into the depths is the one who is enthroned in the heights, 2. the one who delivers from the depths is the one who casts into the depths, 3. the Creator is the Sustainer, the Savior is the Preserver.

The same tendency lies at the basis of all teaching about God, of all dogmatics: the tendency to describe God in the fullness of his being. The category of descriptive praise gives a twofold indication of this.

Praise of God in the fullness of his "being for us" occurs in the development of *one* sentence. This *one* sentence is confession, confession of the one who testifies before the congregation that God has delivered him from the depths. It never lost its connection with declarative, witnessing praise. Only in the late history of the category (see below) was this connection lost.

The description of God's being for us in its fullness remains here still surrounded by praise of God. It cannot be and does not intend to be anything else except praise. It is and knows itself to be an *answer* to the call to praise, with which it is introduced. Here there occurs that to which the one saved calls in Ps. 34:3, "O magnify the LORD with me."

---

declarative: "We have beheld his glory . . . and from his fulness have we all received."

Here the relationship of descriptive to declarative praise may perhaps help us to understand the relationship of proclamation and teaching in the church. Proclamation corresponds to declarative, teaching to descriptive, praise. As in the Psalms descriptive praise lives on declarative (or confessing) praise—the teaching of the church is dependent on proclamation. Just as descriptive praise is development and expansion of the *one* statement in which the one who experienced God's help confesses God's actions before the congregation, so can all teaching, all "dogmatics" of the church be only development of the confession of Jesus as the Christ. Then, however, the teaching of the church can be neither "summa" nor σύστημα (= a compiled whole), but only an explanatory development of the *one* sentence which is not a dogma, but a confession of praise directed toward God. It seems to me that the limit of the "objectivity" of all theological expression lies here. Theology, that is, speaking about God, statements about God, can exist only when surrounded by praise of God. Strictly speaking, God can never become an object. In theology knowledge must never divorce itself from acknowledgment.

5. The Late History of the Category

In the late history of the category we see a remarkable differentiation. On the one side there is a powerful increase of calls to praise, which overrun the Psalm itself, and on the other side a gradual loosening of the ties between descriptive speaking about God and the framework of praise. And it can be shown that the one cannot live without the other. The two statements which form the major section of the descriptive Psalm of praise begin to separate from each other.

1. The one-sided praise of God's grace. Already in the Psalter, Ps. 103 shows a definite preponderance of the praise of God's grace. But precisely this Psalm shows how strongly influenced the praise of the congregation in Israel was by the polarity which has been demonstrated. The singer of this Psalm *wanted* to sing of the grace of God, and yet for him the other side of

this grace is not only there, but this Psalm concludes with praise of the majesty of God, vs. 19, which is then followed in vss. 20-22 by the final call to praise. Moreover, the two expressions of this praise are at least alluded to, the Creator in vs. 14, and the Lord of history in vs. 7.

In the Psalms and prayers of the work of the Chronicler as a rule both statements are there.[88] Ezra 3:11, however, gives as call to praise only the statement of the reason for it, "For he is good, for his steadfast love endures for ever toward Israel." So also 2 Chron. 5:13; 20:21; Jer. 33:11. This sentence plainly became the quintessence of the praise of God altogether, as is shown by its widespread usage. This too is a sign that the one statement, without the corresponding one of praise of God's majesty, continued on. The book of Micah ends in 7:18-20 with praise of the grace of God. Also Luke 1:46-55 shows an absolute preponderance of praise of the goodness of God, but the other side can still be heard in vs. 49.

The Psalms of Solomon show the separation of the motifs very clearly. Typical is 2:33-37, a Psalm complete in itself with a call to praise at the beginning and at the end (33a, 37), the ground for praise, vs. 33b, "For the Lord's mercy [is shown] at the judgment to those who honor him." This is developed in vss. 34-35. Verse 36 repeats 33b, "for the Lord is gracious to those who patiently call on him." The structure is also very simple: a call to praise (imperative) with a broadly developed ground for praise, the content of which, however, is exclusively God's mercy.

The same Psalm shows how a new category develops out of the descriptive Psalm of praise. The grace of God toward his saints means a distinction in the judgment.

> 2:34, "that he separate the pious from the godless, and punish the godless for ever according to their works."
> 35, "and show mercy to the pious because of the oppres-

---

88. Neh. 1:5; 9:6 ff.; 2 Chron. 6:14 f. (each time the introduction of a petition); 1 Chron. 29:10-12 expresses a great number of statements in praise of God's greatness and might only, but in vss. 13-17 there follows praise of God's goodness (which made the people willing to bring an offering).

sion of the godless and repay the godless what he has done to the pious."

All this is intended to be praise of God (see above, vs. 33b), but we sense clearly how the poet tarries here and the contrast of pious and godless becomes an independent theme. The "double wish" of the petition of the individual clearly stands behind this motif. Another example from the Psalms of Solomon, chapter 3,[89] shows how there was further development in this direction.

Verses 1-2 are a reflection which expands a self-exhortation to praise (cf. Ps. 103). That which follows in vss. 3-12, however, is not praise of God, but a contrast of the righteous and the godless. This is probably still intended to be praise of God, for the separation is based (2:33) on God's mercy. But it can really no longer be said that this is speech addressed to God. Without vss. 1-2 this Psalm is a companion piece to Ps. 1.[90]

A further example for the one-sided nature of praise of God is chapter 5:1-2, "O Lord I give praise . . . for thou art gracious."

In vs. 2b a petition is added, which is followed by an alternation of praise and petition. In vss. 9-11 there is praise of the one who sustains, followed again by a petition in vs. 12. Throughout the entire Psalm to vs. 19 the praise remains one-sided.

The other alteration is this: Praise becomes the introduction to a petition, as is general in the Babylonian and Egyptian psalms. A further example of this is Ps. Sol. 18:1-5. Here also there is in vss. 1-4 a long, one-sided praising of God's mercy, preparatory to the petition in vs. 5. So also praise of goodness only is combined with praise of the pious in 10:1-8. The only exception is the concluding doxology in 18:10-12, which probably[91] is a secondary addition here. In it there is one-sided praise of only the Creator: "Great is our God . . . who set the lights in their courses."

89. Gunkel incorrectly separates vss. 1-2 from the rest (*op. cit.,* p. 33). The chapter is a unit.
90. This contrast of righteous and godless is found often in the Ps. Sol.: 4:23-25 (here, like Ps. 1, beginning with "Blessed is . . ."); 6:1-6, only one side, "Blessed is the pious"; 14:1-10 (corresponding to Ps. 1 even in the metaphors!); 15:7-13.
91. So says Kittel on this passage.

In the Ps. Sol. both observations seem to me to stand in relationship to each other, and this is significant for the praise of God as a whole. A displacement can be clearly perceived. The descriptive praise of God loses its polarity (majesty-goodness) and becomes one-sided. Only the goodness of God is praised. The polarity returns, however, in another form, in the contrast of the pious and the godless. To be sure, God's goodness is still praised, but attention is directed much more strongly to the point where now the real tension is seen, that is, no longer in God, but in man, in the contrast of pious and godless. The trace of a deep-going transformation can be seen in this late change in the descriptive Psalms of praise. In the place of God as the sole object in descriptive praise there comes quietly another—the pious man in contrast to the godless man! The loss of the living polarity in the praise of God leads to this gradual shift of attention away from God to the pious man.

2. The one-sided praise of God's majesty. Already in Ps. 150 the ground for the call to praise, which indeed fills the entire Psalm, is only the majesty of God (vs. 2). Alongside this final note of the Psalter we should place the already mentioned concluding doxology of Ps. Sol. 18:10-12. In it also only the greatness of God (specifically, the greatness of the Creator) is praised. 1 Chron. 29:10-12 should also be mentioned. There the praise of God's greatness does not stand entirely by itself, but it is still relatively independent in contrast to what follows.[92]

These are only a few examples of the separation of the praise of God's majesty. It was first completely worked out in the separation of the two developments—as praise of the Creator, and of the Lord of history. These two motifs developed into separate Psalms. Still it is actually only in the creation Psalms that we can speak of the praise of the majesty of God. The historical Psalms consistently unite God's judging and God's saving actions.[93]

92. Jer. 10:6-16 (perhaps without vss. 8-11; cf. Jer. 51:15-19) is almost entirely praise of the majesty of God and praise of the Creator. (An allusion to God's saving action is found in vs. 16.) So also the doxologies in the book of Amos (4:13; 5:8-9; 9:5-6) give together only praise of the Creator, and in one verse (5:9) praise of the Lord of history.
93. Cf. the structure of Ps. 33!

The creation Psalms are the only group of Psalms of praise in the Psalter in which *one* motif developed into an independent Psalm. They are Pss. 8; 19; (29); 104; 139; (148). Each of them is quite distinctive. This group shows that where *one* motif is expanded to form a whole Psalm there is no longer any rigid form.

The clearest similarity to the basic structure of the Psalm of praise is shown by Ps. 8, in which the polarity of God's majesty (vss. 2, 10) and God's grace (vs. 5) still influences the whole of the Psalm. Probably also the bringing together of the two parts of Ps. 19 is intended to move in the direction of this polarity. Ps. 29 also shows the other side in vs. 11.

In the post-canonical Psalms the separating out of one motif goes much further. In Ecclesiasticus there are examples which still show the vitality of that polarity: 15:18-20; 18:1-7. In Ecclus. 39:12-35, God the Creator is praised after an imperative exhortation which is expanded with flowery reflections, vss. 12-15. This song of praise begins and ends,[94] "The works of God are all good." The poet believed he could establish this by observations. Verse 32, "From the beginning I have been convinced, and have thought this out and left it in writing."

Here something else is developed out of praise of the Creator. A turning of attention from God to the creation has been accomplished. That which is praised here is basically no longer creation but nature. It is clear that it is described for its own sake and no longer in its relation to the Creator, in which God alone is to be exalted in such descriptive praise. So then it is also possible for the one praising God to drop out of his role into an easygoing, didactic account, vs. 26, "Basic to all the needs of man's life are water and fire and iron and salt and wheat flour and milk and honey." Then he continues in vs. 28, "There are winds . . ." Alongside this there are other sentences which are moved by God's wonders, such as vss. 19-20, "The works of all flesh are before him, and nothing can be hid from his eyes . . . and nothing is marvelous to him."

94. A double framework! Imperatives in vss. 12-15 and 35; a declaration in vss. 16 and 33.

Also the Odes of Solomon 16 is *only* praise of the Creator, which, even though it contains a very subjective, reflective introduction in vss. 1-5, has in the other verses a manner of speech that is much more disciplined, and much nearer to the O.T., and which remains praise in every line and never turns into verbose description.[95]

Where God the Creator alone is praised, praise can imperceptibly change its object, but will not necessarily do so. It is no longer God who is really being praised, but nature. Ecclesiasticus 39 itself shows that even here a new polarity appears. As among men there are the pious and the godless and there this tension became the theme, so in nature there are adverse happenings and catastrophes in contrast to what is good and wholesome. In vss. 28-31 the poet is concerned specifically with this contrast, and unites it to that of the pious and the godless. All that is adverse exists to punish the godless! In correspondence to this it must be said that all the benefits of nature exist only for the good. For evil men they become harmful, vss. 25, 27.

The other development of the praise of the majesty of God is the praise of God as the Lord of history. A comparison of this motif in the two descriptive Psalms of praise, Ps. 33 and Ps. 136, will show already the expansion and the gradual independence of the motif. In Ps. 33:10-12 (and 16-17) God's activity in history is described only in general and by allusions. In Ps. 136:10-22 a detailed historical report has developed out of it, which recounts the main events from the plagues in Egypt to the conquest of Canaan. It is easy to see that such a historical report could then be separated from the total unit of the descriptive Psalm of praise and become an independent Psalm. Psalm 105 is characteristic of this group. After a long imperative introduction (vss. 1-6) there follows in vss. 7-11, clearly corresponding to the other Psalms of praise, the praise of God as the Lord and Judge (vs. 7), and the praise of the gracious God, the God who entered into a covenant with Israel and who remembers the covenant (vss. 8-11). Then the Psalm tells of God's actions in Israel's history (vss. 12-44).

95. Cf. Ps. Sol. 18:10-12.

The culmination of this historical section is the same as in Ps. 136; the beginning is the life of wandering of the Patriarchs (vs. 12) on the basis of the promise of the land (vs. 11). Psalm 78 also belongs here. The introduction here is not an imperative call to praise; its place has been taken by an introduction in the style of wisdom literature. Still the origin in the descriptive Psalm of praise can be clearly recognized. The theme of the Psalm is "the glorious deeds [*tehillōth*] of the LORD, and his might, and the wonders which he has wrought" (vs. 4). We are dealing, therefore, with praise of the Lord of history. But here something essentially new has been added to the account: it is continued down to the choosing of David (vss. 67-72). The introduction in Deut. 32 is similar. Here the same theme is announced in vs. 3, "For I will proclaim the name of the LORD. Ascribe greatness to our God!" and descriptive praise follows in vs. 4. Next comes the historical account which is continued here to the rejection of Israel by their God, vss. 19-25. But this rejection is not the final happening. Yahweh will "vindicate his people" (vs. 36) and judge their enemies (vss. 40-42). The whole song concludes with an eschatological song of praise (see below), vs. 43. Deuteronomy 32 is the clearest example of how the historical Psalms pass over into eschatological Psalms. Aside from this there are such historical accounts arising out of the praise of God only in mixed forms. Thus it stands together with declarative praise in Exod. 15. The introduction, vs. 2, is similar to the introduction of Deut. 32. The account of Yahweh's deed at the Sea of Reeds, vss. 4-12, is continued down to the conquest, vss. 13-17.

In the lament of the people, a constant element is the looking back to the earlier saving activities of God. This can be expanded into a historical account. This happens above all in Ps. 106, where, alongside the confession of guilt in vss. 6-7, 13-20a, 24-39, there stands the praise of the God, who in spite of all this has helped Israel in a wonderful manner, vss. 8-12, 21b-22, 43-46. Isaiah 63:7-14 is similar. The introduction again resembles Exod. 15:2, but the historical account is here singularly interwoven with the rueful looking back to God's previous deeds of salvation.

In the following section, vss. 14 ff., there is a pleading for deliverance from present need, as at the conclusion of Ps. 106, vs.
47. The historical report with the same motifs reached its greatest
extent, but at the same time passed into an unrestricted report,
in Neh. 9:7-31. In one passage this looking back to God's earlier
deeds of salvation is attached to a lament of the individual, and
here too the historical report can be heard, Ps. 77:15-21. However, the features of the epiphany are predominant here.

A number of the statements of these historical Psalms are encountered in Ps. 81. It begins like the Psalms of praise with an
imperative call to praise, vss. 1-4, and in vs. 5 God's saving deed
in Egypt is given as the basis for the call to praise. In the following, God speaks and reminds Israel of his activity in history, but
also of their disobedience. The Psalm ends in an exhortation to
obedience. God's voice speaks similarly of the history of the
people in Ps. 89:19-37. It is preceded by a complete Psalm of
praise, vss. 5-18, and followed in vss. 38-51 by a lament of the
people. We are dealing here, however, with only one point in
history, the promise to David, which is contrasted with the present time of need.

6. The Eschatological Song of Praise

Gunkel recognized and demonstrated in detail that in Israel,
Psalms and prophecy encountered each other at a definite point
and permeated each other. There is much evidence of this, both
in the prophetic books and in whole groups of Psalms. That this
encounter can only have occurred relatively late is almost self-
evident. The two categories of expression, the prophetic oracle
on the one hand and the speech of the Psalms, which was directed to God, on the other hand, originally had nothing to do
with each other. Each is completely *sui generis*. It is scarcely
imaginable that a mixture of the two categories could have taken
place in their early period. Besides that, however, this mixing is
reflected in the history of prophecy. The first prophet in whose
work the prophetic oracle and the type of speech found in the

Psalms come together strongly and unmistakably is Jeremiah. Although since Mowinckel the mixed forms, thus, e.g., the so-called "enthronement Psalms," have been again attributed to early times, this is in contradiction to the simplest basic literary facts.

Gunkel calls the first group of these mixed forms "eschatological hymns" (Einleitung, pp. 329, 344). The texts which he lists here include many different types. Precisely in this chapter Gunkel proceeds more strongly than elsewhere from the point of view of content: "What makes these hymns eschatological hymns is their content" (p. 344). If, however, we follow Gunkel's correct determination of form (the imperative introduction, and the narrative main section in the "prophetic perfect") then it is not hard to see that here we have an entirely new form. We recognized that the imperative call to praise introduces descriptive praise (see above, p. 102), but originally never declarative praise (or a narrative main section). In the eschatological songs this imperative introduction has been united to a declarative main section, but it is a report that only apparently looks back at something that has already occurred, while in reality speaking of an event that is being announced as if it had already taken place. The introduction of the descriptive Psalm of praise has been combined with the main section of the Psalm of praise of the people, but in so doing the proclamation in the perfect of a coming event has taken the place of God's deed which has already been done.

This perfect of prophetic proclamation, which speaks of God's coming deed of salvation as accomplished, just as the earlier prophetic proclamation of doom anticipated in the proclamation the coming doom as if it had already occurred, is known to us as one of the basic features of the prophecy of Second Isaiah. It is the "perfect of the pronouncement of salvation."[96]

It can scarcely be accidental that the eschatological song of praise in the form described by Gunkel is found most frequently in Second Isaiah. For example,

96. Cf. Begrich, Deuterojesajastudien, p. 9.

Isa. 52:9-10, "Break forth together into singing, you waste places of Jerusalem;

for the LORD has comforted his people, he has redeemed Jerusalem.

The LORD has bared his holy arm before the eyes of all the nations;

And all the ends of the earth shall see the salvation of our God."

Other "eschatological songs of praise" (EP) in Second Isaiah are Isa. 40:9-11; 42:10-13; 44:23; 45:8; 48:20 f.; 49:13; 54:1-2. A thorough investigation of these texts here would lead too far afield. The structure is always the same, with minor variations and expansions (one of these is in Isa. 52:9-10, vs. 10b). It is enough to say here that this form is firmly anchored in the prophecy of Second Isaiah, that these eschatological songs of praise form in several passages the clear conclusion of a larger context,[97] and that in the introductory imperatives the calls to joy are preponderant. It can be assumed that in all probability these songs are a new development made by Second Isaiah. This would then be the form in which in Second Isaiah Psalms and prophecy came to be most closely united. These eschatological songs of praise are to some measure the echo of the community to the promise of salvation which God had made.

This new form is not confined to Second Isaiah, but can be found in various other places. Deuteronomy 32:43 has already been mentioned. There it is the conclusion of a historical Psalm that looks forward to a coming saving action of God, vss. 26-42 (this section is suggestive of many lines in Second Isaiah!). In addition we find it in Isa. 12:4-6 (or 6 alone); 26:4-6 (?); in Jer. 20:13; and 31:7; Ps. 9:12-13 (?); Joel 2:21 (and 23 f. ?); Nah. 2:1 and 3a; Zeph. 3:14-15; Zech. 2:14; 9:9-10.[98]

97. Thus here Isa. 52:9-11 is the conclusion of the composition 51:9–52:12, and 40:9-11 is the conclusion of the prologue.

98. There is also an eschatological song of praise in the supplement to Ps. 69, vss. 32-36, if at the beginning we read (as suggested in the critical apparatus) " 'Look,' ye needy, and 'rejoice,' you who seek God, let your hearts revive. For the Lord 'has heard' the needy, and does not despise his own that are in bonds." In Add. Dan. 1:29-67, vs. 65 has the structure of the EP. Isa. 61:10 must also be

It cannot be asserted with certainty that any of these passages are pre-exilic in origin. In the passages in Jeremiah, Nahum, and Zephaniah we are dealing with later additions, as in Isa. 12. It should not however be asserted as absolutely certain that this eschatological shout of jubilation could not also have been raised before Second Isaiah or at the same period. Still, both historically and theologically and in respect to its occurrence it is firmly anchored in the prophecy of Second Isaiah, in which, even apart from this form, the speech of the Psalms and the words of the prophets came together.

7. Songs of the Enthronement of Yahweh

Alongside the eschatological songs of praise Gunkel places the "Songs of the Enthronement of Yahweh" (*op. cit.,* pp. 329, 345). The problem of these Psalms and the extensive literature concerning them cannot be dealt with thoroughly here. In this connection the work of Kraus, *Die Königsherrschaft Gottes im A.T.,* Tübingen, 1951, should be consulted.[99]

Here I shall only deal with the question of the relation of these Psalms to the previously discussed Psalm categories.

---

reckoned among the eschatological songs of praise. It was intended to be a song of the people, although it is in the singular and has more the character of a PI.

99. In its essentials Kraus's work rests on Gunkel's explanation of the enthronement Psalms and disputes Mowinckel's hypothesis of an early Israelite enthronement festival, to which Mowinckel attributed 46 (!) of the Psalms in the Psalter. He combines Mowinckel's basic material (from the historical accounts in 2 Sam. 6 and 1 Kings 8) with the results of Rost's work on the stories of the ark and deduces on the basis of Ps. 132 a "royal Zion festival," which commemorated every year the two events of 2 Sam. 6 and 7: the choice of Zion and the choice of the house of David. This festival was made meaningless by the exile and then filled with new content by Second Isaiah. Isa. 52:7-10 replaces the choice of the house of David with the proclamation of the dawning of the kingship of God in Jerusalem. The enthronement Psalms are cultic hymns of the thus altered festival.

The essential results of Kraus's work seem to me to prove that Mowinckel's hypothesis, which found such wide acceptance and had such far-reaching consequences, is untenable, and as a result, so is the cultic-mythical interpretation of so many Psalms. Kraus very sharply opposes the more recent representatives of this interpretation, Engnell, Widengren, Bentzen. The main argument against Mowinckel is the demonstration of the dependence of the enthronement Psalms in Second Isaiah.

This critical result is independent of Kraus's assumption of a pre-exilic "royal Zion festival." Here many points must still be dealt with. Basically I can express thankful agreement with his work. Independently of Kraus, whose book I saw only after the conclusion of this work, I myself came to the same conclusion from the point of view of the study of the history of the categories.

The "eschatological song of praise" cited above, Isa. 52:9-10, follows the word of salvation in vss. 7-8. A bearer of glad tidings brings Zion the news that God is (has become) king! This statement corresponds in content to the other portion of the announcement of salvation in the perfect, as in Isa. 43:1. Behind this statement there stands the same event which was the ground for the shout of joy in vss. 9-10 (see above): Yahweh has had mercy on his people (40:2) and by his might destroyed the foe. In and through this he has "become king."[100]

God's kingship is spoken of later in two other eschatological songs of praise: Zeph. 3 and Zech. 9. The same exclamation, "Yahweh has become king," is found in the "enthronement Psalms." It is of decisive importance for the total understanding of these Psalms whether that cry has its origin in the Psalms or in Second Isaiah. It seems to me that the priority of Isa. 52:7-8 can be clearly shown.[101]

I must restrict myself here to presenting the arguments only in the form of theses.

1. In Isa. 52 the exclamation is found in the context where it is a message that has been eagerly awaited and greeted with jubilation, brought by a messenger who comes over the mountains to Jerusalem. In the "enthronement Psalms" the exclamation has become a formula separated from the context.

2. In Isa. 52 Yahweh has become king over and for Israel. In the "enthronement Psalms," as, for example, Ps. 47 shows, he has become king over the nations. The total content of the passages that speak of Yahweh's kingship shows unequivocally that Yahweh was *first* spoken of as King of Israel, and later as king of the nations or king of the entire world.

3. The enthronement Psalms do not constitute a category, nor are the so designated Psalms united by regular marks of a category. Rather, throughout these Psalms we are dealing with mixed forms that are taken from quite varied categories. Also

100. Cf. Kraus, *op. cit.*, pp. 99 ff.
101. So also Baudissin, Κυριος, III, pp. 235 f. For postexilic origin see also Eissfeldt, "Jahweh als König," *ZAW* 46, pp. 81-105. And now, above all, Kraus, *op. cit.*, pp. 99-112.

the corresponding Psalms of the enthronement of an earthly king are missing. Neither can they be reconstructed out of the scattered motifs that are preserved.

4. Aside from the fact that all enthronement Psalms are mixed Psalms, in language and composition they show the marks of a later period.

5. The origin of the motif "Yahweh has become king" in the proclamation of Second Isaiah (whereby a connection with the Babylonian cultic cry is quite possible)[102] and the taking over of this motif into a group of Psalms of the postexilic period can be explained without any difficulty. The opposite explanation is not possible without extensive hypotheses, of which the most weighty and at the same time the most questionable is the assumption of an enthronement festival of Yahweh, which in the O.T. material can be based essentially only on these "enthronement Psalms."

6. In Second Isaiah the exclamation has primarily a historical-eschatological significance and not primarily a cultic one. The so-called enthronement Psalms are evidence that the message proclaimed by Second Isaiah, that Yahweh had become king, was carried on despite the contemporary situation which showed the opposite. This prophetic assurance lived on in the songs of the postexilic community as one of the witnesses in the waiting for something to come.

These theses shall be carried further at only one point, in a short explanation of the "enthronement Psalms."

Their basis is the descriptive Psalm of praise.

Psalm 47 begins with an imperative call to praise, vs. 1; in vs. 2, the reason for the call: praise of the majesty of God; vss. 3-4 develop the theme: he is Lord of history. The imperatives recur in vs. 6, and in vs. 8 the reason given is in the perfect: God has become king. This one-time occurrence is foreign to the original descriptive praise, and cannot be explained as a development out of it. It corresponds exactly, however, to the eschatological song of praise, where too a one-time action of

102. So also Kraus, *op. cit.*, pp. 7 f., 107 f.

Yahweh (as here in the prophetic perfect) is the basis for the imperative call to jubilation.

In addition there are a number of features which are alien to descriptive praise, and which all further expand the description of Yahweh's enthronement: the ascent of the king into his castle after the victory (vs. 5; cf. Ps. 68:18 and many oriental parallels), the clapping of hands (cf. 2 Kings 11:12), and above all the presence of the nations (vss. 1 and 9). These passages above all make it clear that Yahweh's enthronement is not a cultic, but a historical-eschatological act.

Psalm 96. The structure is similar: an introductory call to praise in the imperative, vss. 1-3, based on descriptive praise. In vss. 4-6 God's majesty is described: he is the Creator, vs. 5b. Here too the imperatives are resumed in vss. 7-9 with the message that Yahweh has become king, vs. 10. In vss. 11-12 the imperatives are carried forward with jussives which exhort to joy and jubilation. This is based on the announcement that Yahweh comes (perf.!) to judge the earth. The similarity to the eschatological songs of praise is unmistakable here. Similarly, in Deut. 32 the announcement of the Judge of the world (32:41) follows the historical account. This Psalm is even more clearly eschatological than Ps. 47.

Psalm 98 almost seems to be a variant of Ps. 96. The similarity of these two Psalms makes clear that the cry "Yahweh is king" is not a necessary component of these eschatological Psalms, for it is missing in Ps. 98. In the first part, vss. 1-3, the polarity of descriptive praise of God can be seen in this Psalm. After the imperative call to praise there follows praise of the mighty (vss. 1-2) and of the gracious God (vs. 3). In vs. 3b we have the nations present. As in Ps. 47:4-6 there follow imperatives which exhort to jubilation before God the King. As in Ps. 96, this is continued in jussives, vss. 7-8, which are based on God's coming to judge the world, vs. 9.

While the basic form of descriptive praise is clearly recognizable in these three Psalms, in Pss. 93; 97; and 99 we find various mixed forms. All that these three Psalms have in common is that the cry "Yahweh has become king" is found at the beginning of each of them. While in the previous three Psalms it was prefixed to a whole that was ready at hand, it resulted here in formations that are distinctive, but which have scarcely any traits in common and have extremely loose internal structure.

Psalm 97. The proclamation of the king is first, followed by the exhortation to the world to rejoice. Above all in Ps. 47 this exclamation concerning the king is expanded by the features of the act of enthronement; here it is, however, combined with the description of an epiphany of God, vss. 2-5. This combination is surely secondary. The central part of the Psalm, vss. 6-8, speaks of the forum of this event, vs. 6, and of the effect it has on the foes, vs. 7, and on Zion, vs. 8. The conclusion, vss. 9-12, in content corresponds exactly to a descriptive Psalm of praise, only that the imperative call to praise stands at the end. Verses 9-11 praise God in his majesty, vs. 9, and in his goodness, vss. 10-11. The imperative call to praise at the end is quite surprising. In all other instances where it occurs in this position it resumes the call to praise of the introduction. Psalm 97 is the only Psalm in which it is found only at the end. This alone is a sure sign of the late origin of the Psalm.

Psalm 99. The first verse resembles the first verse of Ps. 97. The composition of the rest of this Psalm, however, is hard to understand, and it has probably not been preserved in its original order. Vss. 5-9 form a complete Psalm of praise. It begins, vs. 5, and ends, vs. 9, with an imperative call to praise. It praises God as the Holy One, vss. 5c and 9b (perhaps 5c should be moved to after 9b), and as the one who forgives, vs. 8b. This praise is expanded in vss. 6-8a by a historical motif: three figures out of Israel's history were in relation to God; they called to him, and he answered them. The expansion of the praise of God is an indication of late origin. This Psalm, complete in itself, was secondarily combined with vss. 1-4, whose order can no longer be clearly recognized. Verse 3, in its present form, can scarcely be the sequel to vs. 2, and vs. 4 also cannot be read in its present form as handed down. The separate statements can all be found in other descriptive Psalms of praise. Outside of vs. 1 there is not a sentence that is reminiscent of the enthronement of Yahweh.

Psalm 93. This Psalm is already different from all others in that the imperative (or jussive) call to praise is totally missing. In fact, there is no framework at all. In vs. 1 the exclamation of kingship is followed immediately by praise of the majesty of God. It is, nevertheless, not descriptive praise that describes the being of God. The expression ". . . is robed, he is girded with strength," is rather the continuation of the exclamation in the perfect in vs. 1. (Cf. the petition in Isa. 51:9, "Put on strength, O arm of the LORD.") The praise of the majesty of God is developed in the usual manner. He is the Creator in vss. 1b-2, and the Lord of history in vss. 3-4. But the two cannot be sharply separated here, for vss. 3-4 are a clear allusion to the primeval struggle with chaos. On the other hand, these sentences remind one of the declarative Psalm of the people, Ps. 124. The chaotic forces which rise up correspond to the historical threat to the people of God. Verse 3 is addressed to Yahweh, almost as a lament of those who are threatened by these powers. Verse 4 corresponds then to the account of deliverance. The fact that God is higher than the highest threats of the force that threatens his people means that salvation is certain. The whole, however, is development of the exclamation of kingship, so that the conclusion of vs. 4 is to be understood in an eschatological sense. This Psalm is truly a unit. The connection of vs. 5 to vss. 1-4 is not clear, but it could easily have originally belonged together with them.

In conclusion, thesis 6 above is confirmed in that there is no proper category of the enthronement Psalms. In Pss. 47; 96; 98, a descriptive Psalm of praise is expanded and modified by the exclamation of kingship. In Pss. 97 and 99 this exclamation has become the chief motif of the Psalm, and yet even in these two the basic category of the descriptive Psalm of praise can be clearly recognized. On the other hand, Ps. 93 is purely an expansion of the exclamation of kingship. Here too there are suggestions of the descriptive Psalm of praise, but the style of the declarative Psalm of praise, transformed into eschatology, is dominant.

The significance of these enthronement Psalms lies in that a motif which was prophetic in origin, the eschatological exclamation of kingship, was absorbed into the descriptive praise of the Psalms. In its original occurrence, Isa. 52, this exclamation was the glad tidings proclaimed to exiled Israel, "Your God reigns!" This message was to assure the exiles of their coming deliverance. Since it lived on after the Exile in the worship of the community, the certainty of the coming intervention of God lived in it, Ps. 96:13, "For he comes to judge the earth." In this prophetic anticipation of Yahweh's coming kingship the expansion of the praise of Yahweh as Lord of history took on the characteristic form for Israel, which had become impotent and was subject to the great powers. It is praise of the Lord of history—in expectation.

In relation to this chapter, cf. D. Michel, "Studien zu den sogenannten Thronbesteigungspsalmen," *VT* 6 (1956), pp. 40-68.

Summary and Conclusion

The two modes of calling on God are praise and petition. As the two poles, they determine the nature of all speaking to God. This is true of all calling on God, in which God stands over against man in a personal relationship. The Psalms from Israel's environment are also to be understood as arising in petition and praise or out of petition and praise, insofar as they are intended as speaking to God or before God. The five basic motifs of the Babylonian psalms are to be explained in terms of this polarity:

I. Address, II. Praise, III. Lament, IV. Petition, V. Vow of Praise.

Calling on God in Israel is identical with that in Babylon not only in the polarity of praise and petition, but also in these five basic motifs. The difference is only in the relationship of these parts to one another. The relation of praise and petition in Babylon is essentially determined by the fact that praise is understood as praise of God *before* the petition, and in part as preparatory for the petition. Praise of God in Israel is essentially praise after the petition has been answered. This determines changes in the basic motifs and in their combinations with each other. The most important of these are as follows: (a) In Babylon there is *one* basic category of Psalms, which contains both praise and petition (and lament) at the same time; in Israel there are *two* basic categories: the Psalm of petition (lament) and the Psalm of praise; (b) The nature of praise of

152

the gods in Babylon is almost always that of descriptive praise. In the O.T. there is both declarative and descriptive praise. Moreover, descriptive praise developed from declarative (or confessing) praise and never entirely lost its connection with it. The vow of praise, which forms in Babylon as well as in Israel the link between lament (and petition) and praise, introduces—in the form of an annunciation in the introduction to the Psalm —descriptive praise in Babylon, but in Israel, declarative praise. Descriptive praise came to have a new introduction in Israel, one entirely lacking in the Babylonian psalms: the imperative call to praise. With this introduction, descriptive praise in Israel became a category in itself. In addition to the (open) Psalm of petition, there is also the petition that has been answered. It is not only certain of being answered, but already testifies to it in declarative praise at the end.

The Categories of the Psalms

The "categories" of the Psalms are not first of all literary or cultic in nature. They are this of course, but it is not the essential element. They designate the basic modes of that which occurs when man turns to God with words: plea and praise. As these two basic modes of "prayer" change and expand, the categories also change and expand. They can travel great distances from this original occurrence, but their origin in it can be recognized in all the branchings of the Psalm categories. There is therefore—often in apparent contradiction to the facts—no Psalm category that arose merely out of some thought concept (such as the theme, nature), or merely out of some cultic exclamation (such as "Yahweh has become king"). Even the Psalms of confidence, the didactic Psalms, and the festival liturgies (such as Ps. 132) are derived in the final analysis from those basic occurrences of plea and praise.

In comparison with the Babylonian psalms it has been shown that the Psalms of the O.T. for the most part fall into *two* basic categories, which correspond to the two basic ways of praying. This work has endeavored to show in the Psalms of the O.T.

the vital, tension-filled polarity of plea and praise. Lay prayer in Israel is also governed by this polarity.[103]

"Cultic prayer" in Israel preserved in astounding measure its connection with lay prayer (in great contrast to Egypt!). In Israel all speaking to God moved between these two poles. There is no petition, no pleading from the depths, that did not move at least one step (in looking back to God's earlier saving activity or in confession of confidence) on the road to praise. But there is also no praise that was fully separated from the experience of God's wonderful intervention in time of need, none that had become a mere stereotyped liturgy.

In view of this polarity, the center of the praise of God in Israel can be seen in declarative (or confessional) praise. It is the center inasmuch as in it (in retrospect of the peril) the danger which has just been overcome still is heard, and is connected to the earnest pleas then made in dire need. It is the center, however, in another entirely different connection. Declarative praise breaks through the boundary between set and free speech (poetry and prose), between the speech of everyday life and the cultic speech of the Psalms. The declarative Psalms of praise have in their simplest form the same structure as the *bārūk* sentences in the historical books. And it is out of the declarative praise of the people that the writing of history in Israel grew.[104]

This work built on Gunkel's demonstration that a Psalm is to be understood only as a branch on the tree of the category; that this tree, moreover, is rooted in a soil, that is, that the Psalm categories are not merely literary categories, but have a Sitz-im-Leben. Gunkel's thesis that the Sitz-im-Leben of the Psalms is the cult is here accepted only conditionally. I have pointed beyond that all too common and indefinite word *cult* to the basic occurrence which transpires in "cult" when men speak to God: the polarity of speaking to God as plea and as praise.

This is the real Sitz-im-Leben of the Psalms. As an occurrence from man to God each Psalm is a unit. Thus its structure can

103. Cf. Wendel, *op. cit.*
104. Cf. in this connection Martin Noth, *Überlieferungsgeschichte des Pentateuch,* Stuttgart, 1948, and my discussion of it in *Zeichen der Zeit,* 1951, p. 10.

be recognized, the structure of a live occurrence. It is a unit, whose members show that they belong to the whole. Never however does this whole become an external scheme, into which a living content is pressed.

Thus the beginnings and transitions to praise of God are seen even in the laments of the people and of the individual. Thus the confession of confidence, which is in Israel such a meaningful and richly developed part, is not to be sharply separated from praise of God. Thus the vow of praise directly points the way to the Psalm of praise.

On the other hand, in the declarative Psalms of praise of the individual and of the people there are echoes of the lament and the pleading of the Psalms of lamentation, and even in the descriptive praise of God, the activity of God, who saves out of the depths, is never forgotten.

Therefore the praise of God in Israel never became a cultic happening, separated from the rest of existence, in a separate realm, that had become independent of the history of the people and of the individual. Rather it occupied a central place in the total life of the individual and the people before God, as for instance the concept of faith does for us. (Cf. Grimme's reference, above, p. 42.) The praise of God occupied for Israel actually the place where "faith in God" stands for us. In Israel it was a fundamental of existence that God was and that therefore they believed in him, and as such it was not disturbed. On this still unshaken basis the clearest expression of the relationship to God was the act of praising God.

This may be shown finally by a peculiar expression of the Psalms concerning praise of God.

THE DEAD DO NOT PRAISE YAHWEH

hōdāh:

> Ps. 6:5, "For in death there is no remembrance of thee; in Sheol who can give thee praise?"
>
> Ps. 30:9, "What profit is there in my death, if I go down to the Pit? Will the dust praise thee? Will it tell of thy faithfulness?"

The Categories of the Psalms

Petition of the people	Declarative praise of the people	Petition of the individual (open)	Petition of the individual (heard)	Declarative praise of the individual	Descriptive Praise
Introductory petition	(Let Israel say so)	Introduction	—		
Lament	Looking back to the time of need ↑ ↓	Lament	Lament		
Confession of confidence	Report of the deliverance ← →	Confession of Confidence	Confession of Confidence		
Petition		Petition	Petition		
(Double wish)		Double wish	(Double wish)		
		(Confidence of being heard)	(Confidence of being heard)		
Vow of praise		Vow of praise	Vow of praise ←	→ Announcement	
				Introductory summary	

Praise (declarative) →	Report of deliverance →	Vow of praise ←	Call to praise →	Praise (descriptive) ←	Praise →	Conclusion
	1. Looking back to the time of need 2. I cried 3. He heard 4. He drew me out				1. Yahweh is great (a) the Creator (b) the Lord of history 2. Yahweh is good (a) he saves (b) he gives bread	

Ps. 88:10, "Dost thou work wonders for the dead? Do the shades rise up to praise thee?"

       11, "Is thy steadfast love declared in the grave, or thy faithfulness in Abaddon?"

Isa. 38:18 f., "For Sheol cannot thank thee, death cannot praise thee; those who go down to the pit cannot hope for thy faithfulness. The living, the living, he thanks thee, as I do this day."

hillēl:

Ps. 115:17, "The dead do not praise the LORD, nor do any that go down into silence. But we will bless the LORD from this time forth, and for evermore."

Isa. 38:18 f., see above.

sippēr:

Ps. 88:11, see above.

Cf. Ps. 118:17, "I shall not die, but I shall live, and recount the deeds of the LORD."

Ps. 119:175, "Let me live, that I may praise thee."

Ecclus. 17:27 f., "Who will sing praises to the Most High in Hades, as do those who are alive and give thanks?" S has instead of this, "For what use to God are all those who have perished in the world, in comparison to those who live and praise him?"

Cf. Erman, *op. cit.,* p. 374; "Hymn to the Sun God":

"All who sleep praise together thy beauty, when thy light shines before their faces . . . When thou hast passed by, so darkness covers them and each one lies down [again] in his coffin."

The vocabulary of praise is found almost always in the vocative. Only in the later period are statements about praise numerous. In the earlier period, apparently the only way in which praise can be spoken of is by calling to give praise. The single, clear exception is this sentence, which is repeated in so many ways and given such emphasis that it must be of especial meaning. And just at this point a sentence from an Egyptian psalm says the exact opposite (see above, p. 50). Reference should be made here to the work of Chr. Barth.[105]

The sentence had its origin in the Psalm of petition of the individual as a motif in support of the petition, which should move God to intervene (Pss. 6; 30; 88). From there it passed over into the declarative praise of the individual, where it was spoken in retrospect, Isa. 38. In the liturgy of Ps. 115 the form can no longer be identified with certainty.

The positive expression of these negative sentences is found in Isa. 38:19, "The living, the living, he thanks thee." The expression "but we" (the *waw*-adversative which indicates the turning point in the petition, see above!) in Ps. 115:18 is to be understood in the same way. Ps. 118:17 and 119:175 express the same thing positively.

All these sentences have the meaning that *only* there, where death is, is there no praise. Where there is life, there is praise.[106]

The possibility that there could also be life in which there was no praise, life that did *not* praise God, does not enter the picture here. As death is characterized in that there is no longer any praise there, so praise belongs to life. The conclusion is not expressed in the O.T., but it must still have been drawn. There cannot be such a thing as true life without praise. Praising and no longer praising are related to each other as are living and no longer living. In the late period the existence of the godless (there is however not yet any name in the O.T. to correspond to it) has become a greater and greater temptation, but the belief is always firmly maintained that such an existence *must* be destroyed by God (Ps. 73). Nowhere is there the possibility of abiding, true life that does not praise God. Praise of God, like petition, is a mode of existence, not something which may or may not be present in life.

That is very hard for us to understand. For us the word has a much too greatly altered, feeble, weakened sound.[107]

---

105. *Die Errettung vom Tode,* esp. p. 151.
106. Cf. Chr. Barth, *op. cit.,* p. 151. "It should be noted, however, that the praise of Yahweh has at the same time the function of a sign of being alive."
107. In the O.T. the verb *hōdāh* has only Yahweh as its object. There is no clear

The essential element of the concept is that of exaltation (see above). The sentence in Isa. 38:9 is also to be heard in this way, "The living, the living, he thanks thee [exalts thee]." In this the whole meaning of the concept the O.T. becomes perhaps somewhat clearer. Exalting is a part of existence. It is so much a part of it, that when one has ceased to exalt God, something else must be exalted. Then God can be displaced by a man, an institution, an idea. Exalting remains a function of existence. World history demonstrates this. Man *must* exalt something, and without such exalting there can apparently be no existence.

But hereby the distance between our present concept "praise" and that of the O.T. is still not shown with sufficient clarity. This "praise" still includes our words "to honor" and "to admire" and "honor" and "admiration." Rilke, for example, felt this when he sought in his concept of "praise" to revive the original, fuller sense and sound of the concept.

Not everywhere where God is no longer truly praised will men of necessity fall into the extremity of the deification of man. But they must surely exalt, admire, honor something. There is no real, full existence that does not in some way honor, admire, look up to something. All this was originally meant in the vocabulary of praise. God is so real, so much alive and mighty for man in the Old Testament that all this is directed toward God. In all ages, however, when this full, living praise turns away from God or becomes withered, thin, and pale, it can be shown how exaltation, admiration, and honor turn away from God to other subjects.

If the praise of God, as the Psalms express it, belongs to existence, then the directing of this praise to a man, an idea,

---

passage in which a man might be the object of *hōdāh*. That the "praise of God" can be completely misunderstood in our modern language is shown by a verse of Hermann Hesse, ("Abends" in *Trost der Nacht,* p. 64):
". . . Summe dumme Gassenlieder
Lobe Gott und mich, . . .
Sage ja zu meinem Herzen
(Morgens geht es nicht),
Spinne aus vergangnen Schmerzen
Spielend ein Gedicht . . ."

or an institution must disturb and finally destroy life itself. The Psalms say that only where God is praised is there life.

PRAISE IN EXPECTATION

The praise of the Old Testament remains in its center, in the declarative praise, a praise in expectation. This is true of the praise of the individual (Job 1:21) as well as of that of the people (the eschatological Psalm). Here and there God is really praised in the midst of trial, but this praise is at the same time a waiting.

We may surmise that the imperative call to praise in the late Psalms is given such great prominence because behind it there is hidden anxiety, whether God will really be praised enough, whether he will be praised aright.

This imperative call to praise, that has such significance for the history of religion,[108] served in its very preponderance as a sign that in this people all voices called for a praise that was yet to be given. This imperative too awaited the fulfilling of praise.

The expectation of the Old Testament is fulfilled in Jesus Christ. So must also the "praise in expectation" be fulfilled in him. The Gospel according to John says in its whole structure that Christ is come to "honor" the Father among men. This *doxazein* can also be translated as "praise."

Christ is come to honor the Father in his life and in his death. At the turning point of his life stands the word, John 17:1, "Father, . . . glorify thy Son that the Son may glorify [=praise] thee." Verse 26, "I made known to them thy name, and I will make it known." Cf. Ps. 22:22, "I will tell of thy name to my brethren." This is the intent of the vow of praise of the Psalms. In the Prologue the work of Jesus Christ is summed up in "The only Son, who is in the bosom of the Father, he has made him known." He has done that which it was the intention of the praise of the people of Israel to do.

108. The caesura between the second and third Babylonian motif of address. See above.

The totally new, the decisive, element lies in the fact that, in contrast to the unanimous declaration of the Psalms, Christ praises the Father through his death, in death. This is the "hour" for which the whole of the Gospel of John waits (John 2; 7; 12; 13; 17).

In that Christ has honored and praised God by his death, the concept of the praise of God has been altered in an essential point. Among the followers of Christ, who honored God by his existence and his death, there is the new possibility of praise by existence (Eph. 1:12), which includes the possibility of praising God through death in following Christ, John 21:19. This is the meaning of a passage which is decisive for the praise of God in the New Testament, John 4:23.[109]

This is also what is meant in Rom. 12:1-2. It has been shown above that the structure of the Letter to the Romans corresponds to that of the declarative Psalm of praise, and Rom. 12:1 ff. corresponds to the vow of praise. The congregation of Jesus Christ is called on to praise God by standing in the world as followers of Jesus Christ, who praised the Father in his life and death. It praises God by confessing in its whole existence "what God has done for us." In such praise of the congregation, in which and by which it confesses before the world God's deed in Jesus Christ, exactly the same thing happens which this investigation established as the basic, central praise of God in the Psalms: declarative praise. The proclamation of the church can then be only a way in which this praise is expressed by the congregation through its existence. It must fail if it sets out to be something else than the *hōdāh* of the one saved in the declarative Psalms of praise. One difference is that the individual no longer proclaims before the congregation, but in the voice of an individual the community proclaims before the world what God has done. The other is that the proper witness to the deeds of God occurs in the existence of the community in the world, and that the proclamation is only a way of bearing this testimony.

109. This proceeds from the exegesis of the concepts *pneuma* and *aletheia*.

Index of Biblical Passages

ISAIAH

168

PRAISE OF GOD IN PSALMS

39 140
39:12-35 139
39:14-35 129
39:16 ff. 127
51 102

ADDITIONS TO
DANIEL

1 132
1:3-5 57
1:17 .... 57, 58
1:22 61
1:26-67 144
1:29 ff. 131, 132
1:32 128
1:65 .... 102, 105
22 60

THE PRAYER OF
MANASSEH

2 127
6-7 127

1 MACCABEES

13:48-51 92

2 MACCABEES

1:24 37
3:30 92
15:34 84

ODES OF
SOLOMON

9:2-11 102
16 140
16:10-19 127
25 102
29 102

PSALMS OF
SOLOMON

2:15-18 58
2:29-31 127
2:31 124
2:33-37 136-137
2:34-37 127
3 137
4:23-25 137
5 137
5:1-2 .... 58, 137
5:5 58
6:1-6 137
7 55
7:4-5 .... 57, 58
7:5 58
7:6-10 81
8:23-26 58
8:33 59
8:34 59
9:1-7 57
9:2-5 58
9:9-11 81
10:1-8 137
13:1-4 ...... 83, 85-86
14:1-10 137
15 105
15:1-3 112
15:1-6 102
15:7-13 137
16 105
16:1-15 102
16:13-15 112
17:1-4 57
18:1-5 137
18:10-12..137, 138, 141

LUKE

1 124
1:46-55 .. 115, 124, 136
1:48 .... 128, 129

1:50 129
1:51-53 124
1:53 118
1:54 129
1:55 129
1:68-75 ...... 84, 115
2:14 129
2:29-32 115

JOHN

1:1-13 133
1:14-18 133-134
2 162
4:23 162
7 162
11:41 74
12 162
13 162
17 162
17:1 161
17:2 161
21:19 162

ACTS

2:11 .... 78, 115
2:24 115

ROMANS

1:14 ff. 116
12:1 ff. 162

EPHESIANS

1:12 162

PHILIPPIANS

2:11 107

Bibliography

PSALM COMMENTARIES AND INTRODUCTIONS

(Superior numerals indicate the edition.)

Olshausen	1853	Wutz	1925
Hitzig[2]	1863-65	Gunkel[4]	1926
Ewald[3]	1866	Gunkel-Begrich (Introduction)	1933
C. B. Moll	1869	König	1926-27
Hupfeld-Nowack[3]	1887-88	Peters	1930
Delitzsch[4]	1883	W. E. Barnes	1931
Kessler[2]	1899	A. Bentzen (Introduction)	1932
Kautzsch	1896	A. Bentzen (Lectures)	1932
Kautzsch[3]	1909	H. Schmidt	1934
Duhm	1899	J. Calès	1936
Baethgen[3]	1904	H. Herkenne HSAT	1936
Ehrlich	1905	J. Hylander	1937
Briggs	1907-09	M. Buttenwieser	1938
Kirkpatrick	1910	W. O. E. Oesterley	1939
Gunkel (Selections)[4]	1917	A. Weiser[2]	1939
Duhm[2]	1922	A. Weiser[3]	1950
Kittel[3-4]	1922	F. Böhl and B. Gemser	1946-49
Kittel[5-6]	1929	B. Eerdmans O.T.S. IV	1947
Bertholet KHSAT	1922	F. Nötscher, Echter-Bibel	1947
Staerk	1911	E. A. Leslie	1949
Staerk[2]	1921	E. Podechard	1949

SURVEYS

The most recent summary presentation of the work on the Psalms:

A. R. Johnson, "The Psalms" in *The Old Testament and Modern Study*, Oxford, 1951. This work gives a comprehensive listing and presentation of the literature in Psalm research in the last twenty-five years. The most recent comprehensive work in the German language is Gunkel-Begrich, *Einleitung in die Psalmen*, 1933.

A slightly older survey is Max Haller, "Ein Jahrzehnt Psalmenforschung, *ThR*, 1929, 6. It gives the literature from 1920-1929.

An important summary of the work on the Psalms is D.C. Simpson,

The Psalmists, Oxford, 1926, with contributions from A. M. Blackman, G. R. Driver, H. Gressmann, T. H. Robinson, W. H. Robinson. For the question of the sacral kingship and its significance for the Psalms, which was not handled extensively here, reference should be made to two surveys: Aage Bentzen, *Messias, Moses redivivus, Menschensohn,* Zürich, Zwingli-Verlag, 1948 (Eng. tr., *King and Messiah,* translated by the author, London: Lutterworth Press, 1955) and Martin Noth, "Gott, König, Volk im A.T.," *Z.Th.K.,* 1950, 2. Cf. H. H. Schrey, "Die alttestamentliche Forschung der sogennanten Uppsala-Schule," *Theol. Zeitschrift,* 7, pp. 321-341, Basel, 1951.

Monographs (Restricted to works important for the theme of this work):

Balla, Emil, *Das Ich der Psalmen,* Göttingen: Vandenhoeck & Ruprecht, 1912.

Barth, Chr., *Die Errettung vom Tode in den individuellen Klage- und Dankliedern des A.T.,* Zollikon: Evangelischer Verlag, 1947.

Baumgartner, W., "Die literarischen Gattungen in der Weisheit des Jesus Sirach," *ZAW* 34, 1914, pp. 161 ff.

Begrich, J., "Die Vertrauensäusserungen im israelitischen Klagelied des Einzelnen und in seinem babylonischen Gegenstück," *ZAW* 46, 1928.

Calès, J., "Les psaumes du règne de Jahwe," *Recherches de science Religieuse* 25, 1935, pp. 462-489, 583-592.

Causse, A., *Die altisraelitische Kultuspoesie und der Ursprung der Psalmen,* 1926.

Causse, A., *Les plus vieux chants de la bible,* Paris: F. Alcan, 1926.

Galling, K., "Der Beichtspiegel, eine gattungsgeschichtliche Studie," *ZAW* 47, 1929, pp. 125 ff.

Gunkel, H., *Einleitung in die Psalmen,* ed. J. Begrich, Göttingen: Vandenhoeck & Ruprecht, 1933.

Gunkel, H., "Psalmen" in *Die Religion in Geschichte und Gegenwart,* Tübingen: Mohr, 1927-1931.

Gunkel, H., "Die israelitische Literatur" in *Kultur der Gegenwart,* ed. Paul Hinneberg, Leipzig: B. G. Teubner, Teil I, Abteilung 7[1], 1906.

Gunkel, H., "The Religion of the Psalms" in *What Remains of the O.T. and Other Essays,* tr. A. K. Dallas, London: Allen & Unwin, 1928.

Gunkel, H., "Die Grundprobleme der israelitischen Literaturgeschichte: Die Psalmen" in *Reden und Aufsätze,* 1913; "Ägyptische Danklieder," *ibid.*

Gunkel, H., "Formen der Hymnen," *ThR* 20, 1917.

Gunkel, H., "Danklieder im Psalter," *Zeitschrift für Missionswissenschaft und Religionswissenschaft,* 34, 1919.

Gunkel, H., "Lieder in der Kindheitsgeschichte Jesu bei Lukas," in *Festgabe für Harnack,* Tübingen: J. C. B. Mohr, 1921.

Horst, F., "Die Doxologien im Amosbuch," *ZAW* 47, 1929.

Jacob, B., "Beiträge zu einer Einleitung in die Psalmen," *ZAW* 16-17, 1897.

Jansen, H. L., *Die spätjüdische Psalmendichtung, ihr Entstehungskreis und ihr Sitz im Leben,* Vidensskapsselskapets Skrifter II, Hist.-filos. Klasse No. 3, 1937.

Löhr, Max, *Psalmenstudien, BWAT,* NF 3, 1922.

Mowinckel, S., *Psalmenstudien,* I-VI, Kristiania, 1921-24.

Mowinckel, S., *Offersang og sangoffer. Salmediktning i Bibelen,* Oslo, 1951 (Eng. tr., *The Psalms in Israel's Worship,* tr. D. R. Ap-Thomas, Oxford: Basil Blackwell, 1962). This book, which brings together the results of Mowinckel's life work on the Psalms, appeared after the conclusion of this present work and I was thus unable to make use of it.

Oesterley, W. O. E., *A Fresh Approach to the Psalms,* N.Y.: Scribners, 1937.

Quell, G., *Das Kultische Problem der Psalmen, BWAT* NF 11, 1926.

Schmidt, H., *Die religiöse Lyrik im A.T.* Tübingen: Mohr, 1912.

Schmidt, H., *Die Thronfahrt Jahwes,* 1927.

Schmidt, H., *Das Gebet der Angeklagten im A.T., BZAW* 49, 1928.

Snaith, N. H., *Studies in the Psalter,* London: The Epworth Press, 1934.

Steuernagel, C., "Psalmen zu einem Thronbesteigungsfest Jahwes?" *Preuss, Kirchenzeitung* 22-24, 1928.

Literature not specifically dealing with the Psalms:

Begrich, J., "Das priesterliche Heilsorakel," *ZAW* 52, 1934.

Begrich, J., *Der Psalm des Hiskia,* Göttingen: Vandenhoeck & Ruprecht, 1926.

Buhl, Frants, "Über Dankbarkeit im A.T. und die sprachlichen Ausdrücke dafür," *Baudissin-Festschrift,* Giessen, 1918, pp. 71-82.

Döller, J., *Das Gebet im A.T. in religionsgeschichtlicher Beleuchtung,* Wien, 1914.

Elbogen, J., *Der jüdische Gottesdienst in seiner geschichtlichen Entwicklung,* Frankfurt, 1924.

Ginsberg, H. L., "Psalms and Inscriptions of Petition and Acknowledgment," in *Louis Ginsberg Jubilee Volume,* N.Y.: American Academy of Jewish Research, 1945.

Glueck, N., *Das Wort hesed im atl. Sprachgebrauch als menschliche und göttliche gemeinschaftsgemässe Verhaltungsweise,* Giessen: A. Topelmann, 1927.

Greiff, A., *Das Gebet im A.T.,* Münster, 1915.

Heiler, F., *Das Gebet,* 2nd ed., München, 1920 (Eng. tr. *Prayer,* tr. Samuel McComb, London: Oxford, 1932).

Hempel, J., *Gebet und Frömmigkeit im A.T.,* Göttingen, 1922.

Hempel, J., "Segen und Fluch im Licht altorientalischer Parallelen," *Zeitschrift der Morgenländischen Gesellschaft,* NF 4, 1925.

Humbert, Paul, *La terouca, analyse d'un rite biblique,* Neuchâtel, 1946.

Humbert, Paul, "Laetari et exultare dans le vocabulaire religieuse de l'ancien testament," *Revue d'histoire et philosophie religieuses.*

Köhler, L., *Deuterojesaja, stilkritisch*

untersucht, Giessen: A. Töpelmann, 1923.

Köhler, L., *Lexikon in veteris testam. Libros,* Leyden: E. J. Brill, 1948-1953.

Nielen, J., *Gebet und Gottesdienst im N.T.,* Freiburg, 1937.

Nöldeke, Th., "Hallelujah," *Baudissin-Festschrift,* Giessen, 1918.

Pedersen, J., *Israel, Its Life and Culture,* I-IV, London: Geoffrey Cumberlege, 1926-1940.

Müller, Christa, *Das Lob Gottes bei Luther,* München, 1934.

Wendel, Adolf, *Das freie Laiengebet im vorexilischen Israel,* Leipzig: Eduard Pfeiffer, 1932.